PALEO
BAKING
at home

The Ultimate Resource for
Delicious Grain-Free Cookies, Cakes,
Bars, Breads *and More*

PALEO
BAKING
at home

MICHELE ROSEN

creator of Paleo Running Momma

PAGE STREET
PUBLISHING CO.

PAGE STREET
PUBLISHING CO.

Copyright © 2020 Michele Rosen

First published in 2020 by
Page Street Publishing Co.
27 Congress Street, Suite 105
Salem, MA 01970
www.pagestreetpublishing.com

Distributed by Macmillan, sales in Canada by The Canadian Manda Group.

24 23 22 21 20   2 3 4 5 6

ISBN-13: 978-1-62414-937-5
ISBN-10: 1-62414-937-5

Library of Congress Control Number: 2019942509

Cover and book design by Kylie Alexander for Page Street Publishing Co.
Photography by Michele Rosen

Printed and bound in the United States

To Diana, Emily and Drew—my favorite
taste testers and kitchen companions. And to
my husband, Adam, for always making
me feel like a baking rock star!

CONTENTS

INTRODUCTION

I have lots of early childhood memories involving my favorite foods, but while testing the recipes for this book, I kept flashing back to one in particular. I must have been about three years old and it was the first time I was baking chocolate chip cookies with my mom. Now, my mom is not much of a baker, so this was a rare occasion in both of our lives! I can still feel the excitement, wondering whether it was *really* possible to make cookies—*cookies*—from practically nothing. I remember looking up at her as she took careful steps to do everything right—correct measurements, mixing the dough the right way, scooping the right amount and so on. The cookies were good, *but* they browned too much on the bottom (seriously—I remember this!) and I knew in that moment that (1) baking is *truly* magical and (2) there are *always* going to be ways to improve the outcome! In hindsight, that was the moment when I officially became a "recipe tester."

Throughout my childhood, my mom gave me lots of freedom to experiment with anything I wanted to in the kitchen—from attempting to make my own peanut butter *without* a food processor (not recommended!) to attempting to make soft pretzels from Wonder Bread (just me?) to countless attempts to make the "perfect" chocolate chip cookie, to a pretty intense cheesecake phase when I baked a different flavor of cheesecake nearly every day. As I got older, my love for baking and cooking only developed further and I enjoyed preparing food and desserts for every social event, birthday, holiday and, really, just because I felt like it. Even though I enjoy cooking as well, baking will always have my heart and the magic never seems to fade.

When I started eating a Paleo diet several years ago for health reasons, I never doubted that I would find ways to re-create my favorite treats. However, writing this book has proven to me once again that it's absolutely possible to use Paleo-friendly, real-food ingredients to bake anything. My blog, Paleo Running Momma, has been an outlet for me to share all my experiments in Paleo cooking and baking, and I love hearing how it's become a go-to resource for many people looking to re-create their favorites with better-for-you ingredients.

Each recipe in this book is free of grains, gluten, legumes and refined sugar. Many recipes are completely dairy-free, and in others I use ghee (a type of clarified butter) as an alternative to butter. The lactose and casein are removed in the process of making ghee, so it's suitable for many people who typically avoid dairy. Some recipes will give you the option to use either ghee, grass-fed butter or palm oil shortening.

In several recipes, you have the option to use either maple or coconut sugar inter-changeably. I like to think of maple sugar as "light brown sugar" and coconut sugar as "dark brown sugar," because the biggest difference they create is in the color of the final product. I tend to stick to maple sugar for anything light in color and use coconut sugar when I don't mind a darker brown color, or when baking with chocolate. I personally prefer the flavor and color of maple sugar, which is why I often list it first, and I encourage you to try it as well!

My goal is for this cookbook to become your go-to resource for any kind of baked treat you crave! You'll find everything from classic chocolate chip cookies to holiday favorites, such as double-crust apple pie and cutout sugar cookies, to authentic soft pretzels and New York–style bagels that completely wowed my whole family. I sincerely hope that these recipes bring you and your family lots of joy, and of course, a little bit of magic.

PALEO BAKING PANTRY STAPLES AND EQUIPMENT

Since I bake all the time, I make sure I have my most frequently used ingredients and equipment at my fingertips, ready to go for a spin whenever I feel like creating something yummy! These lists are not completely exhaustive, but do cover most of what you'll need to make any recipe in this book, along with a few tips that will help you have the most success with Paleo baked goods.

Pantry Staples

The following list is a guide to the most frequently used ingredients throughout this book. Having your pantry well stocked means you can whip up any recipe when a craving hits!

Flours: The flours I use in this book are blanched almond flour, tapioca flour (see Note), coconut flour and golden flaxseed meal. The majority of the recipes use almond flour or a combination of almond and tapioca flours, and a few use coconut flour as well. These flours each have distinct properties and purposes and cannot be subbed in for one another, so having them all handy means you'll be covered for anything you want to bake. I buy all my flours from Amazon and love the brands Oh! Nuts and Anthony's Goods.

Each grain-free flour lends its own unique properties to Paleo baking, which is why I often combine flours to attempt to mimic the texture of traditional baked goods. While blanched almond flour is almost the "perfect" flour for grain-free baking, it works extremely well with tapioca and/or arrowroot flour to give breads, cakes and muffins "fluff," cookies a nice chewy texture and pastry, a crisp, flaky texture.

Note: I often use tapioca flour and arrowroot flour interchangeably in Paleo baking and, for the most part, they can sub in seamlessly for each other. The exception to this rule for me is when using larger amounts of the flour (1 cup [112 g] or more) in which case I've found tapioca lends a superior texture. I always choose tapioca flour over arrowroot for such recipes as piecrusts, bagels and pretzels, for the best texture.

Fats: Refined coconut oil and ghee are the most frequently used Paleo-friendly fats you'll see in this book. If you are okay with using grass-fed butter, it can nearly always sub in for ghee. However, subbing in coconut oil for recipes that call for ghee often causes problems with the resulting texture. I use refined over unrefined (virgin) coconut oil only to avoid the strong coconut flavor of unrefined coconut oil, but using it won't affect the texture, only the flavor, of the final product.

I also use palm oil shortening as an option in my frosting and pastry recipes since it's solid, light in color and creamy at room temperature. If you decide to use palm oil shortening for your piecrusts, make sure you buy one that's not mixed with coconut oil, since that will create a crumbly piecrust.

Sweeteners: I do not have a "favorite" Paleo sweetener, as each has its own unique properties that make it special. I use maple sugar the most often since it has a wonderful flavor and is light in color like cane sugar. It's also very easy to blend into a powder to make icings and frostings. I always buy A&A maple sugar from Amazon. You'll also find I use coconut sugar, pure maple syrup and raw honey. With the exception of maple sugar, all can now be easily found at most grocery stores. If you can't find maple sugar, coconut sugar is nearly always a good substitute.

Powdered Sugar: Making powdered sugar from maple or coconut sugar is surprisingly easy, and it's the base for many of the frostings and icings in this book. Simply blend your sugar in a NutriBullet (what I use), high-speed blender or food processor until it has a powdery consistency. You'll want to measure the sugar after blending to make sure you're adding the right amount.

Milk and Cream: For the most part, full-fat coconut milk is used most frequently throughout this book. I use the canned, full-fat version (unless noted otherwise) and always make sure the cream and water are blended before measuring for recipes. For coconut cream, you can either buy cans of coconut cream only, or use the thick part of a chilled can of coconut milk and discard the water. In general, I prefer buying coconut cream separately, as I find it works much better for whipped cream and ensures it's not mixed with too much water.

Leavening: Baking soda is the main leavening agent I use in my recipes. For recipes where baking powder is preferred, you can either use aluminum-free baking powder or make your own Paleo-friendly (corn-free) baking powder (see below). There are only two recipes in the book that use yeast.

To make grain-free baking powder, combine 2 teaspoons (6 g) of cream of tartar with 1 teaspoon of baking soda. Use just 1 teaspoon of the mixture for these recipes.

Nut Butters: Several of my cookie recipes use smooth almond butter to lend a great chewy texture and subtle nutty flavor. Although I typically specify almond butter, you can sub in any smooth nut or seed butter in these recipes.

Chocolate Chips: Most store-bought chocolate chips (even dairy- and soy-free ones) contain cane sugar, which is technically a refined sugar and therefore not a part of the Paleo diet. If you're okay with a little cane sugar in your chocolate chips, feel free to use any dark chocolate ones you like (Enjoy Life makes great ones!). For a fully Paleo option, you can buy Hu Kitchen dark chocolate bars (Whole Foods Market carries them). Simply chop them up and add them to any recipes that call for chocolate chips or chunks. Hu Kitchen also makes dark chocolate Paleo "gems" that are perfect when a recipe calls for chocolate chips or chunks.

Other Mix-Ins: A variety of nuts and dried fruit are used throughout the book. Most are easy to find without any added sugar, but for those that typically have added sugar (such as cranberries), I always buy fruit-sweetened brands from Amazon. I also use unsweetened coconut flakes and shredded coconut in a few recipes, which you can typically find at the grocery store near the grain-free flours.

Cooking Sprays: Luckily, it's easy to find Paleo-friendly cooking sprays at most grocery stores now, made with coconut or avocado oil. I like to use these as backup to grease my cake pans after lining with parchment paper, and also for donut pans and muffin cups.

Flavorings: I mostly use organic vanilla extract in my recipes; however, some recipes call for pure almond extract or fruit juices and zests, such as lemon, lime or orange. Freshly squeezed is always best when it comes to fruit juice!

Equipment

Although no fancy equipment is needed for most of the recipes in this book, some things make Paleo baking a lot easier.

Parchment Paper and Parchment Muffin Liners: Paleo recipes often tend to stick more than their traditional versions, so lining your baking sheets, pans and muffin cups with parchment paper is extremely helpful to ensure your baked goods will release! If you have trouble finding parchment muffin liners in stores, check out Amazon—it's where I get mine.

Electric Hand Mixer: This makes all the difference for creaming together ingredients for frosting, cookie dough and cake batter.

High-Speed Blender: This is what makes it possible to make smooth Paleo frostings and icings, since it can turn maple or coconut sugar into powdered sugar in a few seconds! It also makes cashew-based frostings like a champ. For small batches, I always use my NutriBullet, but for larger batches of cashew frosting, I use a Vitamix.

Food Processor: I don't ever make a Paleo piecrust without my food processor! It does an incredible job of pulsing the dough ingredients just right in a matter of seconds. I also use it to chop nuts, and it can also be used to make cashew frostings (although I prefer a blender for this, personally).

Stand Mixer: Although no recipes in this book fully require a stand mixer, it does mix together the bagel and pretzel dough quickly and easily, and can also be helpful in place of an electric hand mixer.

DECADENT
CAKES *and*
CUPCAKES

I used to think that sticking to a grain-free, Paleo diet meant I couldn't have "real" cake. Boy, was I wrong! While all the ingredients in these cakes are from wholesome, real-food sources, the texture and flavors are reminiscent of all your old favorites.

These Paleo cakes and cupcakes are rich and moist, with the perfect amount of sweetness! The frostings are made without confectioners' sugar or butter, yet they're rich, creamy and picky-eater approved.

They're perfect for those special occasions when you want to share a healthier sweet treat that everyone will still love. From classic carrot cake (page 21) to decadent Double Chocolate Frosted Layer Cake (page 25) to snickerdoodle cupcakes (page 35), there's something to suit everyone's cravings.

SIMPLY VANILLA LAYER CAKE WITH VANILLA FROSTING

I have to admit that when it comes to cake, I'm a kid at heart and vanilla is my favorite. I perfected this triple-layer cake, complete with a moist, tender crumb and fluffy buttercream frosting that's sweetened with raw honey but tastes like the real thing, according to my kids. It's surprisingly easy to make and perfect as a birthday cake. Try garnishing it with berries for an extra pop of color and flavor.

Yield: One 8" (20-cm) triple-layer cake

CAKE

Coconut or avocado oil spray

2¾ cups (264 g) blanched almond flour

½ cup (56 g) tapioca flour

1 tsp baking soda

½ tsp fine sea salt

4 large eggs, at room temperature

6 tbsp (90 ml) full-fat coconut milk, blended prior to adding

6 tbsp (90 ml) melted coconut oil, cooled to almost room temperature

1 cup (156 g) pure maple sugar

1 tbsp (15 ml) fresh lemon juice

2 tsp (10 ml) pure vanilla extract

FROSTING

¾ cup (134 g) palm oil shortening, at room temperature

½ cup (98 g) ghee, at room temperature

½ cup (56 g) tapioca flour

½ cup (170 g) raw honey

¼ tsp fine sea salt

2 tsp (10 ml) pure vanilla extract

Prepare the cake: Preheat your oven to 350°F (177°C). Line three 8-inch (20-cm) cake pans with parchment paper and spray with coconut or avocado oil spray.

In a medium-sized bowl, combine the almond and tapioca flours, baking soda and salt.

In a separate large bowl, whisk together the eggs, coconut milk, coconut oil, maple sugar, lemon juice and vanilla until very smooth. Whisk the dry mixture into the wet until well combined.

Divide the cake batter evenly among the prepared pans and bake for 20 minutes, or until golden brown. A toothpick inserted in the center of a layer should come out clean.

Remove the cakes from the oven and allow the layers to cool for 15 minutes in the pans, then carefully remove and let cool on wire racks.

While the cakes cool, prepare the frosting: In a large bowl, combine the palm oil shortening, ghee, tapioca flour, honey and salt. With an electric hand mixer, beat on medium speed until smooth and creamy. Mix in the vanilla and continue to beat for another minute, or until very smooth and creamy. Chill the mixture in the refrigerator while waiting for the cake layers to cool. Just make sure you allow it to sit at room temperature for about 15 minutes, or until spreadable, before frosting the cake.

Once the cake layers are completely cooled, place 1 layer, rounded side down, on a cake stand or turntable. Spread with the frosting, then cover with a second layer and repeat. Add the third layer, rounded side up. Frost the top and sides of the cake as desired.

Store leftover cake, covered, in the refrigerator for up to 4 days.

CREAMY LEMON CURD LAYER CAKE WITH LEMON BUTTERCREAM FROSTING

I'm a lemon lover through and through, and lemon curd is one of my greatest Paleo discoveries.
Between the creamy, tangy curd, moist, brightly flavored lemon cake and lemon buttercream
frosting, you have a lemon masterpiece here! Since the lemon curd needs to be thoroughly
chilled before spreading over the cake, it's best to prepare it the day before and chill it overnight,
or up to 48 hours in advance. The leftover lemon curd is perfect to spread
on muffins or serve as a dip with fruit.

Yield: One 8" (20-cm) triple-layer cake

LEMON CURD

3 large eggs

½ cup (119 ml) fresh lemon juice (from 3 to 4 lemons)

1 tbsp (6 g) lemon zest (from about 1 medium-sized lemon)

6 tbsp (128 g) raw honey

⅛ tsp sea salt

⅓ cup (65 g) ghee or grass-fed butter, at room temperature

CAKE

Coconut or avocado oil spray

4 large eggs

6 tbsp (90 ml) fresh lemon juice

Zest of 2 lemons

⅓ cup (79 ml) melted ghee

1½ tsp (8 ml) pure vanilla extract

1 tsp pure almond extract

1 cup (156 g) pure maple sugar

2¾ cups (264 g) blanched almond flour

½ cup (56 g) tapioca flour

¾ tsp baking soda

½ tsp fine sea salt

Prepare the lemon curd: In a medium-sized saucepan, whisk together the eggs, lemon juice and zest, honey and salt, using a wire whisk.

Place over medium heat and continue to whisk while cooking for about 30 seconds, or until the honey has melted and all is combined. Still whisking, add the ghee and lower the heat to medium-low. Continue to cook, whisking, until the mixture is creamy and thickens enough to coat the back of a spoon. (There will be lumps. Don't worry, we will remove them!)

Immediately remove the saucepan from the heat and very slowly pour the curd through a mesh strainer into a glass bowl. Since it's thick, you'll have to use a whisk to help things along through the strainer. Allow the curd to cool for about 30 minutes, then chill in the refrigerator until cool and thick. You will need ½ cup (112 g) of this, total, for the cake; save the rest for another use.

Prepare the cake: Preheat your oven to 350°F (177°C), line three 8-inch (20-cm) cake pans with parchment paper and spray with coconut or avocado oil cooking spray.

In a large bowl, whisk together the eggs, lemon juice and zest, ghee, vanilla, almond extract and maple sugar until well combined and smooth.

In a separate bowl, combine the almond and tapioca flours, baking soda and salt, then stir the dry mixture into the wet until well integrated.

Spread the batter equally among the prepared cake pans and bake for 18 to 22 minutes, or until set in the center and beginning to turn golden brown. A toothpick inserted in the center of each of the layers should come out clean.

(continued)

CREAMY LEMON CURD LAYER CAKE
WITH LEMON BUTTERCREAM FROSTING (CONT.)

FROSTING

½ cup (89 g) palm oil shortening, at room temperature

¼ cup (49 g) ghee, at room temperature but solid

¼ cup (28 g) tapioca or arrowroot flour

½ cup (170 g) raw honey (a thick, creamy honey works best)

½ tsp pure vanilla extract

Zest of 1 lemon

1 tbsp (15 ml) fresh lemon juice

⅛ tsp fine sea salt

½ tsp pure lemon extract (optional)

Remove from the oven and allow the layers to cool for about 15 minutes in the pans before carefully turning onto wire racks to cool completely. I recommend refrigerating the layers for about 15 minutes before filling and icing.

While the cakes cool, prepare the frosting: In a large bowl, combine the palm oil shortening, ghee, tapioca flour and honey. With an electric hand mixer, beat on medium speed until smooth and creamy. Mix in the vanilla, lemon zest and juice, salt and lemon extract (if using), and continue to beat for another minute, or until very smooth and creamy. Chill the mixture in the refrigerator until you're ready to frost the cake, or use right away.

Place 1 layer of cake, rounded side down, on a cake plate or turntable, then spread about ¼ cup (56 g) of the chilled lemon curd over the top, starting in the center and working outward, leaving 1 inch (2.5 cm) around the edge, since it will ooze out a little. Place a second layer over the first and repeat. Save any remaining lemon curd for another use.

Place the third layer, rounded side up, over the curd and frost the top and sides with the chilled lemon buttercream. You can serve immediately or store, loosely covered, in the refrigerator until you're ready to serve. I like this cake best after it's chilled for several hours, since it gives the lemon curd a chance to set.

Store leftovers in the refrigerator for up to 5 days.

CARROT CAKE WITH PINEAPPLE AND "CREAM CHEESE" FROSTING

Whether you love carrot cake or not, you're going to go wild for this one! The perfectly moist, sweet, warmly spiced Paleo carrot cake with a cream cheese frosting made from cashews is finally here. This is a recipe that is great to spread out over a couple days. You can soak the cashews while you chill your coconut cream for the frosting. And, while not necessary, you can make the frosting a day ahead of time and allow it to chill and thicken up in the refrigerator overnight.

Yield: One 8" (20-cm) triple-layer cake

FROSTING

2½ cups (375 g) unsalted cashews, soaked in water for a minimum of 2 hours

⅔ cup (203 g) coconut cream, chilled

3 tbsp (42 g) coconut oil, solid

3½ tbsp (53 ml) fresh lemon juice

½ cup (170 g) raw honey

1 tsp pure vanilla extract

¼ tsp fine sea salt

CAKE

Coconut oil spray

2¾ cups (264 g) blanched almond flour

½ cup (56 g) tapioca flour

1 tsp baking soda

1 tsp aluminum-free baking powder or homemade Paleo baking powder (see page 12)

½ tsp fine sea salt

2 tsp (4 g) ground cinnamon

1 tsp ground ginger

½ tsp ground nutmeg

CAKE (CONT.)

½ tsp ground cloves

½ cup (119 ml) melted refined coconut oil

⅔ cup (151 g) coconut sugar

⅓ cup (79 ml) pure maple syrup

4 large eggs

2 tsp (10 ml) pure vanilla extract

⅔ cup (150 g) crushed pineapple, drained and excess juice squeezed out

2 cups (260 g) grated carrots (3 to 4 large carrots)

1½ cups (170 g) chopped pecans, divided

Prepare the frosting: In a high-speed blender (such as a Vitamix) or food processor, blend all the frosting ingredients well until smooth and creamy. Chill the frosting for at least an hour before using it.

Prepare the cake: Preheat your oven to 350°F (177°C) and line three 8-inch (20-cm) round cake pans with parchment paper on the bottom, then spray the bottom and sides with coconut oil spray.

In a medium-sized bowl, combine the almond and tapioca flours, baking soda, baking powder, salt, cinnamon, ginger, nutmeg and cloves, then set aside.

In a larger bowl, using an electric hand mixer, beat together the coconut oil, coconut sugar, maple syrup, eggs, vanilla and pineapple on medium-low speed. Add the dry mixture to the wet and beat on low speed until fully combined and a thick batter forms. By hand, gently fold in the grated carrots and half of the pecans.

(continued)

CARROT CAKE WITH PINEAPPLE AND "CREAM CHEESE" FROSTING (CONT.)

Divide the batter equally among the prepared cake pans, scraping the bowl to use all the batter.

Bake for 18 to 20 minutes, or until a toothpick inserted in the center of each layer comes out clean.

Remove from the oven and allow to cool in the pans for 30 minutes, then carefully remove from the cake pans and transfer to wire racks to cool completely to room temperature before frosting.

Frost the cake with the chilled frosting between the layers and over the top as you desire, and garnish with the remaining pecans.

Store leftovers, covered, in the refrigerator for up to 1 week.

Note: In addition to chilling the frosting overnight, you can also refrigerate the cake layers for easier frosting. The cake can be frosted a day ahead of time—I actually like it better this way! Just remember to leave the cake out for an hour before serving, to return to room temperature.

DOUBLE CHOCOLATE FROSTED LAYER CAKE

This classic chocolate layer cake has gotten nothing but rave reviews from everyone who tries it, and it's also a favorite for my family as well. This rich, decadent, moist and tender cake is made healthier with a blend of grain-free flours, organic coconut oil and unrefined coconut sugar. The dairy-free buttercream frosting is out of this world delicious and *none* of it tastes Paleo, even though it totally is!

Yield: One 8" (20-cm) triple-layer cake

CAKE

Coconut or avocado oil spray

1½ cups (144 g) blanched almond flour

⅓ cup (37 g) tapioca flour

⅓ cup + 1 tbsp (40 g) raw cacao powder

1 tsp baking soda

¼ tsp fine sea salt

4 large eggs, at room temperature

½ cup (119 ml) unsweetened almond milk, at room temperature

1 cup (226 g) coconut sugar

½ cup (119 ml) melted coconut oil, cooled

2 tsp (10 ml) pure vanilla extract

Prepare the cake: You can make this cake in three 8-inch (20-cm) layers (what I did) or two 9-inch (23-cm) layers. Baking times will vary slightly, so watch for doneness.

Preheat your oven to 350°F (177°C). Line your cake pans with parchment paper and spray with coconut or avocado oil spray.

In a large bowl, combine the almond and tapioca flours, cacao powder, baking soda and salt, then set aside.

In a separate large bowl, whisk together the eggs, almond milk, coconut sugar, coconut oil and vanilla until very smooth. Immediately add the dry mixture and stir well (you can also use an electric mixer) until a smooth batter forms.

Divide the batter evenly among the prepared cake pans and place on the middle racks of your oven (nearer to the top is preferred). Bake for 15 to 25 minutes, depending on your choice of cake pans; the cake is done once the center is set and a toothpick inserted near the center of a layer comes out clean or with a dry crumb.

Remove from the oven and let the cake layers cool on wire racks while you prepare the frosting.

(continued)

DOUBLE CHOCOLATE FROSTED LAYER CAKE (CONT.)

CHOCOLATE BUTTERCREAM FROSTING

½ cup (89 g) palm oil shortening

½ cup (108 g) coconut oil, solid but softened slightly

1 cup (226 g) powdered coconut sugar or maple sugar (see page 12)

½ cup (50 g) raw cacao powder

3 tbsp (45 ml) unsweetened almond or coconut milk, divided

1 tsp pure vanilla extract

⅛ tsp fine sea salt

Prepare the frosting: In a medium-sized bowl, use an electric hand mixer (or a stand mixer) to beat together the palm oil shortening and coconut oil until mostly smooth and fluffy. Add your powdered sugar of choice and the cacao powder and continue to beat, then add 2 tablespoons (30 ml) of the almond milk and continue to beat. Add the vanilla, salt and the last tablespoon (15 ml) of the almond milk slowly to reach the desired consistency.

Assemble the cake: To make the cake easier to frost, chill the cooled layers first for 15 to 30 minutes. The frosting will be creamy at room temperature; it will harden quickly if chilled, but you can easily rebeat it to a creamy consistency if you'd like to store it in the fridge while the cake chills.

Carefully place 1 layer of cake, rounded side down, on a cake stand, turntable or plate. Using an offset spatula or butter knife, frost the top of the first layer, then place a second cake layer on top and repeat. Repeat with the third layer of cake, rounded side up, and frost around the outside of the cake as desired.

Store leftovers, covered, in the refrigerator for up to 4 days.

APPLE RAISIN SPICE CAKE WITH HONEY CASHEW FROSTING

When fall rolls around, I want nothing more than to bake sweet, warmly spiced apple goodies! This supermoist spiced apple raisin cake is dangerously addicting—I can attest to that! No matter the season, you're going to fall in love with all the flavors and textures in this cake. The frosting—just like the carrot cake frosting (page 21)—is easiest to work with when it's chilled overnight. You can also make and frost the cake a day ahead of time, simply leaving it out for an hour before serving to return to room temperature.

Yield: One 8" (20-cm) double-layer cake

FROSTING

2¼ cups (338 g) unsalted cashews

¼ cup (45 g) palm oil shortening or refined coconut oil, solid

½ cup (170 g) raw honey

2 tbsp (30 ml) fresh lemon juice

1 tsp pure vanilla extract

⅛ tsp fine sea salt

CAKE

Coconut oil spray

2¾ cups (264 g) blanched almond flour

½ cup (56 g) tapioca flour

1 tsp baking soda

½ tsp aluminum-free baking powder or homemade Paleo baking powder (see page 12)

½ tsp fine sea salt

2 tsp (4 g) ground cinnamon

1 tsp ground ginger

½ tsp ground nutmeg

½ tsp ground cloves

CAKE (CONT.)

½ cup (119 ml) melted refined coconut oil, cooled

¾ cup (170 g) coconut sugar

¼ cup (85 g) raw honey

½ cup (125 g) unsweetened applesauce

4 large eggs

2 tsp (10 ml) pure vanilla extract

1 cup (120 g) peeled and grated apples (about 2 apples), squeezed well between paper towels to remove excess water (measure after squeezing)

½ cup (75 g) raisins

Chopped walnuts, for garnish

Prepare the frosting first so it can chill while you make the cake: In a high-speed blender (such as a Vitamix) or food processor, blend all the frosting ingredients well until smooth and creamy. Chill the frosting for at least an hour before using it, or up to overnight.

Prepare the cake: Preheat your oven to 350°F (177°C) and line two 8-inch (20-cm) round cake pans with parchment paper on the bottom, then spray the bottom and sides with coconut oil spray.

In a large bowl, combine the almond and tapioca flours, baking soda, baking powder, salt, cinnamon, ginger, nutmeg and cloves.

(continued)

APPLE RAISIN SPICE CAKE
WITH HONEY CASHEW FROSTING (CONT.)

In a separate large bowl, use an electric hand mixer or stand mixer on low speed to combine the coconut oil, coconut sugar, honey and applesauce for a minute or so. Then, beat in the eggs and vanilla until well combined. Add the dry mixture and continue to beat on low speed until fully combined. By hand, stir in the grated apples and raisins to evenly distribute in the batter.

Divide the batter evenly between the prepared cake pans, smoothing the tops gently. Bake for 25 to 30 minutes, or until set in the center and browning around the edges. A toothpick inserted in the center of a layer should come out with a dry crumb.

Remove from the oven and allow the cakes to cool in the pans on a wire rack for about 30 minutes, then carefully remove from the pans and let cool completely on the wire racks before frosting.

Frost the cake with the chilled frosting, between the layers and over the top or as you desire. Sprinkle the top with chopped walnuts, for serving.

Store leftovers, covered, in the refrigerator for up to 1 week. Any leftover frosting can also be stored in the refrigerator for up to 1 week.

PUMPKIN SPICE CUPCAKES
WITH MAPLE CINNAMON FROSTING

Anything pumpkin brings back all the warm feels from childhood when there was no day better than Thanksgiving Day! These dreamy cupcakes are perfectly comforting and fun to make with the kids, too. Whether it's the holiday season or not, it's hard to resist the sweet pumpkin spices and maple cinnamon frosting that make these cupcakes special.

Yield: 12 cupcakes

CUPCAKES

3 large eggs

1 cup (227 g) organic pure pumpkin puree

¼ cup (59 ml) canned full-fat organic coconut milk, blended prior to adding

½ cup (113 g) organic coconut sugar or maple sugar

2 tbsp (30 ml) melted refined coconut oil or ghee

1 tsp pure vanilla extract

1¾ cups (168 g) blanched almond flour

¼ cup (28 g) tapioca or arrowroot flour

¾ tsp baking soda

2 tsp (4 g) pumpkin pie spice

1 tsp ground cinnamon

¼ tsp fine sea salt

FROSTING

½ cup (89 g) palm oil shortening, at room temperature

½ cup (98 g) ghee

¼ cup (28 g) tapioca flour

¾ cup (117 g) powdered maple sugar (see page 12)

FROSTING (CONT.)

1 tsp pure vanilla extract

2 tsp (4 g) ground cinnamon

⅛ tsp fine sea salt

Prepare the cupcakes: Preheat your oven to 350°F (177°C) and line a 12-well muffin pan with parchment liners.

In a large bowl, whisk together the eggs, pumpkin puree, coconut milk, coconut sugar, coconut oil and vanilla until very smooth.

In a separate bowl, combine the almond and tapioca flours, baking soda, pumpkin pie spice, cinnamon and salt well, then stir the dry mixture into the wet until fully combined.

Spoon in the batter to fill each prepared muffin well about three-quarters full. Bake for 20 minutes, or until a toothpick inserted in the center of a cupcake comes out clean or with a dry crumb.

Remove from the oven and allow the cupcakes to cool in the pan for 10 minutes, then transfer to wire racks to cool completely.

Meanwhile, prepare the frosting: In a large bowl, combine the palm oil shortening, ghee, tapioca flour and powdered maple sugar. With an electric hand mixer, beat on medium speed until smooth, then add the vanilla, cinnamon and salt and continue to beat until creamy.

Pipe or spread the frosting onto the completely cooled cupcakes before serving.

Store leftovers, covered, in the refrigerator for up to 5 days.

TRIPLE CINNAMON COFFEE CAKE

Coffee cake is one of my favorite things to bake—and eat—and I wanted to go all out with cinnamon flavor for this one! This coffee cake is perfect for an afternoon snack, dessert and—okay, fine, breakfast, too!

Yield: One 8" (20-cm) square cake (about 9 servings)

CINNAMON SUGAR

3 tbsp (42 g) coconut sugar

2 tsp (4 g) ground cinnamon

CINNAMON STREUSEL

½ cup (48 g) blanched almond flour

⅓ cup (75 g) coconut sugar

1½ tsp (3 g) ground cinnamon

⅛ tsp fine sea salt

¼ cup (49 g) ghee or coconut oil, solid, broken into pieces

COFFEE CAKE

3 large eggs, at room temperature

¼ cup (59 ml) canned full-fat coconut milk, blended

1 tbsp (15 ml) fresh lemon juice

¼ cup (59 ml) melted refined coconut oil

½ cup (113 g) coconut sugar

¼ cup (39 g) pure maple sugar

1 tsp pure vanilla extract

2 cups (192 g) blanched almond flour

¼ cup (28 g) tapioca or arrowroot flour

½ tsp baking soda

¼ tsp fine sea salt

2 tsp (4 g) ground cinnamon

ICING

⅓ cup (52 g) powdered maple sugar (see page 12)

½ tsp ground cinnamon

½ tsp pure vanilla extract

3–4 tsp (15–20 ml) coconut or unsweetened almond milk

Preheat your oven to 350°F (177°C) and line an 8-inch (20-cm) square cake pan with parchment paper.

Prepare the cinnamon sugar: In a small bowl, combine the coconut sugar and cinnamon and set aside.

Prepare the streusel: In a separate small bowl, mix together all the streusel ingredients with a fork or pastry blender until thick crumbs form, then chill until you're ready to use it.

Prepare the cake: In a large bowl, whisk together the eggs, coconut milk, lemon juice, coconut oil, coconut and maple sugars and vanilla until very smooth.

In a separate medium-sized bowl, combine the almond and tapioca flours, baking soda, salt and cinnamon. Stir the dry mixture into the wet, using a spoon or spatula, until well combined.

(continued)

TRIPLE CINNAMON COFFEE CAKE (CONT.)

Transfer half of the batter to the prepared cake pan, then sprinkle with the cinnamon sugar and top with the remaining batter, scraping the sides of the bowl. Spread out evenly in the pan, then sprinkle all of the streusel over the top. Bake for 28 to 30 minutes, or until a toothpick inserted near the center of the cake comes out clean or with a dry crumb.

Remove from the oven and allow the cake to cool in its pan on a wire rack for about 20 minutes. Carefully remove the cake from the pan and transfer it to the wire rack.

While the cake cools, prepare the icing: Whisk together the powdered maple sugar, cinnamon, vanilla and coconut milk, adding the coconut milk slowly until you get the right consistency for drizzling. Drizzle the icing over the partially cooled cake and serve slightly warm or at room temperature.

Leftovers can be stored, loosely covered, at room temperature for up to 3 days, then covered, in the refrigerator, or frozen, to keep longer.

SNICKERDOODLE CUPCAKES
WITH CREAMY CINNAMON FROSTING

While testing recipes for this book, I discovered that my husband had no idea what snickerdoodles are. With a fluffy, soft texture and classic sweet cinnamon flavor, these cookie-inspired cupcakes are a fun alternative when you want a little something extra! Baked with a layer of cinnamon sugar in the middle and topped with a dreamy cinnamon frosting, they're perfect for holiday gatherings or whenever a major cinnamon craving hits.

Yield: 12 cupcakes

CUPCAKES

3 large eggs, at room temperature

⅓ cup (79 ml) canned full-fat coconut milk, blended prior to adding

⅓ cup (79 ml) melted coconut oil, cooled to almost room temperature

1½ tsp (8 ml) pure vanilla extract

¾ cup (117 g) pure maple or coconut sugar, or a combination of the two

1¾ cups (168 g) blanched almond flour

⅓ cup (37 g) tapioca flour

¾ tsp baking soda

½ tsp cream of tartar

1 tbsp (6 g) ground cinnamon

¼ tsp fine sea salt

CINNAMON SUGAR

3 tbsp (29 g) pure maple sugar

1 tbsp (6 g) ground cinnamon

Prepare the cupcakes: Preheat your oven to 350°F (177°C) and line a 12-well muffin pan with parchment liners.

In a large bowl, whisk together the eggs, coconut milk, coconut oil, vanilla and maple sugar.

In a separate bowl, combine the almond and tapioca flours, baking soda, cream of tartar, cinnamon and salt, then stir the dry mixture into the wet until fully combined.

Prepare the cinnamon sugar: In a small bowl, combine the maple sugar and cinnamon.

Using a spoon, fill each prepared muffin well about three-quarters full, sprinkle each batter portion with ½ teaspoon of the cinnamon maple sugar mixture, then cover with the remaining batter. Sprinkle the remaining cinnamon sugar over the top, then bake for 18 to 20 minutes, or until set and a toothpick inserted in the center of a cupcake comes out clean.

Remove from the oven and allow the cupcakes to cool in the pan for 10 minutes, then transfer to wire racks to cool completely.

(continued)

SNICKERDOODLE CUPCAKES
WITH CREAMY CINNAMON FROSTING (CONT.)

CINNAMON FROSTING

½ cup (89 g) palm oil shortening, at room temperature

½ cup (98 g) ghee

¼ cup (28 g) tapioca flour

¾ cup (117 g) powdered maple sugar (see page 12)

1 tsp pure vanilla extract

2 tsp (4 g) ground cinnamon

⅛ tsp fine sea salt

Meanwhile, prepare the frosting: In a large bowl, combine the palm oil shortening, ghee, tapioca flour and powdered maple sugar. With an electric hand mixer, beat on medium speed until smooth, then add the vanilla, cinnamon and salt and continue to beat until creamy.

Pipe or spread the frosting onto the completely cooled cupcakes before serving.

Store leftovers, covered, in the refrigerator for up to 5 days.

ICED LEMON POPPY SEED BUNDT CAKE

This cake surprised me in the very best way possible. I loosely based the recipe on the lemon poppy seed muffins on my blog, but took everything to the next level. It has a buttery flavor, thanks to ghee, and great rise, thanks to using both baking soda and baking powder. Plus, I just couldn't say no to a maple lemon icing drizzled all over the cake before serving—I mean, can we ever say *no* to icing?!

Yield: One 10" (25-cm) Bundt cake

CAKE

Coconut oil spray

⅓ cup (65 g) ghee, at room temperature

¾ cup (117 g) pure maple sugar

5 large eggs, at room temperature

¼ cup (59 ml) coconut or unsweetened almond milk

½ cup (119 ml) fresh lemon juice

Zest of 2 lemons

1 tsp pure vanilla extract

1 tsp pure almond extract

2¾ cups (264 g) blanched almond flour

½ cup (56 g) tapioca flour

1 tsp aluminum-free baking powder or homemade Paleo baking powder (see page 12)

½ tsp baking soda

½ tsp fine sea salt

3 tbsp (24 g) poppy seeds

ICING

½ cup (78 g) powdered maple sugar (see page 12)

1 tbsp (15 ml) fresh lemon juice

Prepare the cake: Preheat your oven to 350°F (177°C) and spray a 10-inch (25-cm) Bundt pan with coconut oil spray.

In a large bowl, cream together the ghee and maple sugar until smooth, then beat in the eggs, coconut milk, lemon juice and zest, vanilla and almond extract.

In a separate large bowl, stir together the almond and tapioca flours, baking powder, baking soda and salt, then slowly beat the dry mixture into the wet. By hand, fold in the poppy seeds until evenly distributed.

Transfer the mixture to the prepared pan and smooth the top. Bake for 35 minutes, or until golden brown on top and a toothpick inserted near the center of the cake comes out clean.

Remove from the oven and allow the cake to cool in the pan for 15 minutes, then carefully transfer to a wire rack set over a piece of parchment paper.

While the cake cools, prepare the icing: In a small bowl, whisk together the powdered maple sugar and lemon juice, adding the juice slowly until you get the right consistency for drizzling. Drizzle the icing over the partially cooled cake and allow the icing to harden before serving.

Serve slightly warm or at room temperature.

Store leftovers at room temperature for the first 2 days, or cover and refrigerate for up to 5 days.

DOUBLE STRAWBERRY CUPCAKES

The strawberry flavor is over the top in these cupcakes and my family went absolutely wild for them! With a reduced strawberry puree added to the batter plus freeze-dried strawberries to flavor and color the frosting, they're every berry lover's dream.

Yield: 16 cupcakes

STRAWBERRY PUREE
1 lb (455 g) fresh strawberries

CUPCAKES
2½ cups (240 g) blanched almond flour

½ cup (56 g) tapioca flour

1 tsp baking soda

½ tsp fine sea salt

2 large eggs

2 large egg whites

3 tbsp (45 ml) canned full-fat coconut milk, blended prior to adding

3 tbsp (45 ml) melted coconut oil, cooled to almost room temperature

1 cup (156 g) pure maple sugar

1 tsp pure vanilla extract

1–2 tbsp (3–4 g) ground freeze-dried strawberries

FROSTING
1 cup (178 g) palm oil shortening or grass-fed butter, at room temperature

½ cup (170 g) raw honey

⅛ tsp fine sea salt

⅓ cup (37 g) tapioca flour

1 cup (20 g) freeze-dried strawberries, blended to a powder

Prepare the strawberry puree: In a blender, puree the fresh strawberries. Transfer the puree to a medium-sized saucepan and bring to a boil, then lower the heat to medium-low. Simmer, stirring occasionally, for 25 minutes, or until you're left with ⅔ cup (155 g) of puree. Remove from the heat and allow to cool completely before using in the cake batter—chilling it in the refrigerator is fine.

Prepare the cupcakes: Preheat your oven to 350°F (177°C) and line 16 wells of two muffin pans with parchment liners.

In a medium-sized bowl, combine the almond and tapioca flours, baking soda and salt.

In a separate large bowl, whisk together the eggs, egg whites, coconut milk, coconut oil, maple sugar and vanilla until very smooth. Whisk the dry mixture into the wet until well combined, then stir in the ⅔ cup (155 g) of strawberry puree, followed by the freeze-dried strawberry powder.

Using a spoon, fill each prepared muffin well about three-quarters full. Bake for 18 to 20 minutes, or until a toothpick inserted in the center of a cupcake comes out clean.

Remove from the oven and allow to cool in the pans for 10 minutes, then transfer to wire racks to cool completely before frosting.

While the cupcakes cool, prepare the frosting: In a large bowl, combine the palm oil shortening, honey, salt and tapioca flour. With an electric hand mixer, beat on medium speed until smooth and creamy. Add the freeze-dried strawberry powder and continue to beat until the frosting is evenly pink.

Once completely cooled, frost the cupcakes as desired to serve.

Store leftovers, covered, in the refrigerator for up to 4 days.

IRRESISTIBLE COOKIES

Baking cookies at home was always one of my favorite pastimes, and the reason I started to love baking to begin with. Is there really anything better than a fresh batch of soft chocolate chip cookies? Thankfully, there's no need to sacrifice texture or flavor when making Paleo versions of your favorite cookies. From chewy and crisp to soft and pillowy, these recipes provide everything you're craving while keeping it grain-free and Paleo.

Even better—these recipes are perfect for kids to help out with or even make by themselves. Most recipes don't require a mixer at all; a few just need an electric hand mixer.

This chapter is filled with my personal favorites, including my Chewy "Oatmeal" Raisin Cookies (page 48), such seasonal gems as Soft and Chewy Gingerbread Cookies (page 66) and Perfect Cutout Sugar Cookies (page 47) and even cookies with a twist, such as Lemon Poppy Seed Cookies with Lemon Icing (page 70) and Orange Coconut Cookies (page 51). Oh, and I just had to throw in a Giant Fudgy Chocolate Chip Skillet Cookie (page 65), too—maybe my favorite recipe of all!

ULTIMATE PALEO
CHOCOLATE CHIP COOKIES

Chocolate chip cookie recipes aren't hard to find, but there are some that clearly stand out above the rest! This is one of the best—they have the perfect chewy texture and a slight nutty flavor that makes them totally irresistible and lovable to all.

Yield: 16 to 18 cookies

1¼ cups (120 g) blanched almond flour

¼ cup (28 g) tapioca or arrowroot flour

½ tsp baking soda

¼ tsp fine sea salt

⅓ cup (85 g) smooth almond or cashew butter

⅓ cup (79 ml) melted coconut oil, cooled

¼ cup (59 ml) pure maple syrup

¼ cup (39 g) pure maple or coconut sugar

1 tsp pure vanilla extract

1 large egg yolk

1 cup (170 g) Paleo-friendly dark chocolate chips or chopped dark chocolate

Preheat your oven to 350°F (177°C) and line a large baking sheet with parchment paper.

In a medium-sized bowl, whisk together the almond and tapioca flours, baking soda and salt, then set aside.

In a separate large bowl, using an electric mixer or whisk, blend together the nut butter and coconut oil until smooth, then add the maple syrup, maple sugar and vanilla and continue to mix until very smooth. Add the egg yolk and continue to beat on low speed or whisk until fully combined. Using a spoon, slowly mix in the dry mixture until a sticky cookie dough forms. Fold in the chocolate chips, then chill the mixture in the fridge for 10 minutes.

Using a 1½-tablespoon (23-ml) cookie scoop, drop the mixture about 2 inches (5 cm) apart onto the prepared baking sheet. Press down gently on each mound—but not too much since they will still spread out in the oven. Bake for about 10 minutes, or until the cookies are set in the center and beginning to brown around the edges. They will be very soft, but don't overbake them so their texture remains chewy.

Remove from the oven and allow to cool on the baking sheet for about 5 minutes, then carefully transfer to wire racks to cool completely.

Store the cookies, loosely covered, at room temperature for up to 4 days.

PERFECT CUTOUT SUGAR COOKIES

I've tested tons of Paleo sugar cookie recipes, and these are *by far* the best ones—crisp and slightly chewy. The dough is easy to work with as far as grain-free dough goes and is perfect for holiday decorating! For a true white icing, you can sub in organic powdered sugar for the powdered maple sugar. For pink icing, just blend up some freeze-dried strawberries and stir a bit of the powder into the white icing.

Yield: 12 to 16 cookies

COOKIES

6 tbsp (73 g) ghee, at room temperature

6 tbsp (59 g) pure maple sugar

1 tsp pure vanilla extract

1 large egg, at room temperature

2 cups (192 g) blanched almond flour

¼ cup (28 g) tapioca flour

¼ tsp baking soda

¼ tsp fine sea salt

ICING

¾ cup (117 g) powdered maple sugar (see page 12)

1 tbsp (15 ml) coconut or unsweetened almond milk

½ tsp pure vanilla extract

Prepare the cookies: In a large bowl, cream together the ghee and maple sugar, using an electric hand mixer. Add the vanilla and egg and continue to mix until smooth. Stir or mix in the almond and tapioca flours, baking soda and salt until a dough forms. Gather the dough into a ball and flatten into a disk. Wrap it in plastic wrap, then chill in the refrigerator for 2 hours or overnight.

Preheat your oven to 350°F (177°C) and line a large baking sheet with parchment paper.

Place the dough on a separate sheet of parchment paper and roll out to ½-inch (1.3-cm) thickness. Use cookie cutters to cut your preferred shapes, then place about 1 inch (2.5 cm) apart on the prepared baking sheet.

Bake for 8 to 10 minutes, or until the cookies just begin to turn light brown. Remove from the oven and allow to cool for 5 minutes on the baking sheet, then transfer to wire racks to cool completely.

Repeat the steps with the remaining cookie dough, chilling the dough in between batches if it becomes too sticky.

While the cookies cool, prepare the icing: In a small bowl, whisk all the icing ingredients together and drizzle over the cooled cookies.

Store, loosely covered, at room temperature for the first day, then cover and refrigerate for up to 5 additional days.

CHEWY "OATMEAL" RAISIN COOKIES

Although I'm a chocolate lover through and through, there is something so homey and comforting about a chewy oatmeal raisin cookie. Even without the oats, these cookies provide all the same warm, cozy feelings! With a crisp outside and chewy middle, a nutty cinnamon flavor and sweet, chewy raisins throughout, they'll fool everyone in the best way. You can even stir in coconut flakes to mimic the texture of rolled oats. Either way, they're truly the ultimate Chewy "Oatmeal" Raisin Cookies.

Yield: 12 or 13 cookies

1¼ cups (120 g) blanched almond flour

¼ cup (28 g) tapioca flour

½ tsp baking soda

¼ tsp fine sea salt

1½ tsp (3 g) ground cinnamon

¼ cup (63 g) smooth almond butter

⅓ cup (72 g) refined coconut oil, soft but solid

⅓ cup (79 ml) pure maple syrup

1 tsp pure vanilla extract

1 large egg yolk

MIX-INS

⅓ cup (50 g) raisins

⅓ cup (25 g) unsweetened coconut flakes (optional)

Preheat your oven to 350°F (177°C) and line a large baking sheet with parchment paper.

In a medium-sized bowl, whisk together the almond and tapioca flours, baking soda, salt and cinnamon and set aside.

In a separate large bowl, using an electric mixer, cream together the almond butter and coconut oil until smooth, then add the maple syrup and vanilla and continue to mix until very smooth. Add the egg yolk and beat on low speed until fully combined.

Using a spoon, slowly mix in the flour mixture until a sticky cookie dough forms, then fold in the raisins and coconut flakes (if using). Chill the dough in the refrigerator for 10 to 15 minutes.

Using a 1½-tablespoon (23-ml) cookie scoop, scoop the mixture onto the prepared baking sheet, about 2 inches (5 cm) apart, since they will spread a bit. Bake for 9 to 11 minutes, or until the cookies are set in the center and beginning to brown around the edges.

Remove from the oven and allow to cool on the baking sheet for about 5 minutes, then carefully transfer to wire racks to cool completely.

Store, loosely covered, at room temperature for up to 3 days, or store in the refrigerator for up to 1 week.

ORANGE COCONUT COOKIES

These chewy cookies are packed with citrus flavor, thanks to both orange juice and zest in the dough. Add coconut flakes and you have a cookie reminiscent of a tropical drink! These are fun to make when you're craving a unique cookie with fresh and bright flavors.

Yield: 14 to 16 cookies

---

1 cup + 2 tbsp (108 g) blanched almond flour

¼ cup (28 g) tapioca or arrowroot flour

½ tsp baking soda

¼ tsp fine sea salt

½ tsp ground cinnamon

⅓ cup (59 ml) melted ghee

¼ cup (63 g) smooth almond or cashew butter

¼ cup (85 g) raw honey

¼ cup (39 g) pure maple sugar

1 large egg yolk

1½ tbsp (23 ml) fresh orange juice

Grated zest of 1 orange

1 tsp pure vanilla extract

⅔ cup (50 g) unsweetened coconut flakes

Preheat your oven to 350°F (177°C) and line a large baking sheet with parchment paper.

In a medium-sized bowl, combine the almond and tapioca flours, baking soda, salt and cinnamon and set aside.

In a separate large bowl, whisk or use an electric hand mixer to blend together the ghee, almond butter, honey and maple sugar until smooth, then add the egg yolk, orange juice and zest and vanilla. Continue to mix until smooth. Stir the dry mixture into the wet until well combined, then stir in the coconut flakes.

Use a 1½-tablespoon (23-ml) cookie scoop to drop the dough 2 inches (5 cm) apart onto the prepared baking sheet, then press each mound down slightly in the center. Place on a rack in the upper portion of the oven and bake for 9 to 10 minutes, or until set and turning golden brown.

Remove from the oven and allow the cookies to cool for 5 minutes on the baking sheet, then transfer to wire racks to cool completely.

Store, loosely covered, at room temperature for up to 4 days.

CHOCOLATE-DIPPED COCONUT MACAROONS

In my opinion, macaroons simply need to be dipped in chocolate, period. I grew up eating lots of different varieties—chocolate chip, plain, double chocolate—but the chocolate-dipped ones were always the ones I craved. Since this healthy homemade version can be delicate, using a spoon to carefully dip them into the melted chocolate is essential.

Yield: 24 cookies

MACAROONS
4 large egg whites

½ cup (170 g) raw honey

¼ tsp fine sea salt

3 cups (225 g) unsweetened finely shredded coconut

½ tsp pure vanilla extract

½ tsp pure almond extract

CHOCOLATE SHELL
2 cups (340 g) Paleo-friendly chopped dark chocolate or dark chocolate chips, or from-scratch chocolate shell that follows

1 tsp coconut oil

OR

FROM-SCRATCH CHOCOLATE SHELL (OPTIONAL)
⅔ cup (158 g) coconut oil

⅔ cup (67 g) raw cacao powder or unsweetened cocoa powder (sift first if very lumpy)

⅓ cup (79 ml) pure maple syrup

½ tsp pure vanilla extract

⅛ tsp fine sea salt

Prepare the macaroons: Preheat your oven to 325°F (163°C). Line 2 baking sheets with parchment paper.

In a large bowl, using an electric mixer, beat the egg whites on high speed until stiff peaks are formed, about 3 minutes. Add the honey and salt and continue to beat on medium speed until fully combined, then stir in the shredded coconut, vanilla and almond extract.

Using a 1½-tablespoon (23-ml) cookie scoop, scoop the coconut mixture 2 inches (5 cm) apart onto the prepared baking sheets, making sure each scoop is tightly packed so the cookies don't fall apart.

Baking 1 batch at a time for even browning, bake in the upper two-thirds of your oven for 15 to 17 minutes, or until set and lightly browned. Remove from the oven and allow the macaroons to cool completely on the lined pan. Once cooled, line a baking sheet that has not been used to bake them with a clean piece of parchment paper and carefully transfer the macaroons to the fresh paper.

Make the chocolate shell using either the chocolate chip method or the from-scratch method that follows.

To prepare the chocolate chip–based shell: In a microwave-safe glass bowl, combine the chocolate and coconut oil and melt in 30-second increments in a microwave, stirring after each increment, until fully melted.

(continued)

CHOCOLATE-DIPPED
COCONUT MACAROONS (CONT.)

To prepare the from-scratch chocolate shell: In a small saucepan over very low heat, whisk together the coconut oil, cacao powder and maple syrup until the coconut oil has melted and a smooth, shiny mixture forms; this only takes a minute or two. Remove from the heat and stir in the vanilla and salt. Allow to sit at room temperature for 5 to 10 minutes, long enough to let the chocolate thicken up a bit for dipping.

To dip the macaroons: Use a spoon to carefully dip the bottom of each macaroon in the melted chocolate and place, chocolate side down, back on its freshly lined baking sheet. Drizzle the remaining chocolate over the tops as desired. Chill the baking sheet in the refrigerator for about 20 minutes, or until the chocolate is firm.

The macaroons can be stored at room temperature or chilled for up to 1 week.

CHOCOLATE-DIPPED ALMOND SHORTBREAD COOKIES

These cookies scared me at first, because it's tough to make grain-free cookies without a binder, such as an egg or egg replacement. However, they really surprised me with how true to texture and flavor they are to traditional shortbread. I highly recommend chilling these in the refrigerator to firm them up before dipping them in the chocolate, since they're delicate. My kids swore they were eating bakery cookies—they couldn't believe they were homemade and Paleo!

Yield: 18 to 20 cookies

SHORTBREAD COOKIES

¾ cup (146 g) ghee, at room temperature

⅔ cup (104 g) pure maple sugar

1 tsp pure almond extract

2 cups (192 g) blanched almond flour

2 tbsp (14 g) tapioca flour, plus more for sprinkling

¼ tsp fine sea salt

CHOPPED CHOCOLATE SHELL

1 cup (170 g) Paleo-friendly chopped dark chocolate or from-scratch dipping chocolate that follows

FROM-SCRATCH CHOCOLATE

⅔ cup (158 g) coconut oil

⅔ cup (67 g) raw cacao powder or unsweetened cocoa powder (sift first if lumpy)

⅓ cup (79 ml) pure maple syrup

½ tsp pure vanilla extract

⅛ tsp fine sea salt

Prepare the cookies: In a large bowl, using an electric hand mixer, cream together the ghee and maple sugar. Add the almond extract, then stir in the almond and tapioca flours and salt and mix until fully combined. Wrap the dough in plastic wrap and chill it in the refrigerator for 30 minutes, or until you can work with it easily.

Preheat your oven to 300°F (149°C) and line a large baking sheet with parchment paper. Place the dough on a separate large sheet of parchment paper dusted with tapioca flour and place another sheet of parchment on top.

Roll out the dough into a rectangle about ½ inch (1.3 cm) thick and use cookie cutters, a pizza cutter or a sharp knife to cut into 1 x 3–inch (2.5 x 7.5–cm) rectangles. Carefully place them at least 1 inch (2.5 cm) apart on the prepared baking sheet, then bake for 20 minutes, or until beginning to turn light brown.

Remove from the oven and allow the cookies to cool completely on their pan.

Make the dipping chocolate using either the chopped chocolate method or the from-scratch method that follows.

To prepare the chopped chocolate for dipping: In a microwave-safe glass bowl, melt the chocolate in the microwave in 30-second increments, stirring between each increment, until melted and smooth.

(continued)

CHOCOLATE-DIPPED ALMOND SHORTBREAD COOKIES (CONT.)

To prepare the from-scratch chocolate for dipping: In a small saucepan over very low heat, whisk together the coconut oil, cacao powder and maple syrup until the coconut oil is fully melted and a smooth, shiny mixture forms; this takes about a minute or two. Remove from the heat and stir in the vanilla and sea salt. Allow to sit at room temperature for 5 to 10 minutes, long enough to let the chocolate thicken up for dipping.

To dip the cookies: Once the cookies have cooled, carefully dip half of each in the chocolate, then place them back on their baking sheet, far enough apart to not touch. Allow the chocolate to cool before serving. These cookies have the best texture when they're chilled slightly in the refrigerator.

Store, covered, in the refrigerator for up to 1 week.

CHUNKY MONKEY COOKIES

The chunky monkey combination isn't just for ice cream (although I'll never argue against the ice cream flavor—it's genius!). These cookies bring the "chunky monkey" title to life with lots of chopped dark chocolate and walnuts stirred into a cookie dough made with bananas and almond butter. They have a unique flavor and soft texture reminiscent of banana bread that's hard to beat!

Yield: 20 to 22 cookies

⅔ cup (200 g) mashed banana (2 small or 1 large)

½ cup (125 g) smooth almond butter

⅓ cup (52 g) pure maple or coconut sugar

1 tsp pure vanilla extract

1¾ cups (168 g) blanched almond flour

1 tsp ground cinnamon

½ tsp baking soda

¼ tsp fine sea salt

½ cup (85 g) Paleo-friendly chopped dark chocolate

½ cup (57 g) chopped walnuts (optional)

Preheat your oven to 350°F (177°C) and line a large baking sheet with parchment paper.

In a large bowl, combine the mashed banana, almond butter, maple sugar and vanilla, then whisk or use an electric hand mixer to beat until smooth.

In a separate medium-sized bowl, combine the almond flour, cinnamon, baking soda and salt, then add the dry mixture to the wet and stir until a sticky dough forms. Fold in the chocolate and walnuts (if using).

Using a 1½-tablespoon (23-ml) cookie scoop, scoop 20 to 22 mounds of dough onto the prepared baking sheet and gently press each mound down in the center. Bake for 10 to 11 minutes, or until set and turning light brown.

Remove from the oven and allow the cookies to cool for 10 minutes on the baking sheet, then carefully transfer them to wire racks to cool completely.

Store leftovers, loosely covered, at room temperature for up to 4 days to maintain their texture.

DOUBLE CHOCOLATE
CHERRY COOKIES

Dried cherries simply aren't used often enough in cookies! I'm not sure anyone can argue the chocolate–cherry combination—it offers the best mix of rich dark chocolate flavor and sweet, tangy, chewy cherries that works perfectly in a good cookie. Plus, whether you're craving chocolate or fruit, whipping up a batch of these is always the answer!

Yield: 12 to 14 cookies

¾ cup (72 g) blanched almond flour

2 tbsp (14 g) tapioca flour

½ cup (50 g) raw cacao powder, sifted

½ tsp baking soda

¼ tsp fine sea salt

⅓ cup (79 ml) melted coconut oil, cooled

¼ cup (63 g) smooth almond butter

¼ cup (59 ml) pure maple syrup

¼ cup (57 g) coconut sugar

1 tsp pure vanilla extract

1 large egg yolk

½ cup (85 g) Paleo-friendly dark chocolate chips

½ cup (75 g) dried tart cherries, roughly chopped

Preheat your oven to 350°F (177°C) and line a large baking sheet with parchment paper.

In a large bowl, combine the almond and tapioca flours, cacao powder, baking soda and salt, then set aside.

In a separate large bowl, whisk together the coconut oil, almond butter, maple syrup and coconut sugar until smooth. Add the vanilla and egg yolk and continue to whisk until smooth, then stir in the dry mixture until fully combined. Gently stir in the chocolate chips and cherries to evenly distribute. Chill the dough in the fridge for 5 to 10 minutes.

Using a 1½-tablespoon (23-ml) cookie scoop, scoop the dough about 2 inches (5 cm) apart onto the prepared baking sheet, then press down gently on each mound. Bake for 8 to 10 minutes, or until the cookies are set and their tops are bumpy.

Remove from the oven and allow the cookies to cool on the baking sheet for 5 minutes, then carefully transfer to wire racks to cool completely.

Store, loosely covered, at room temperature for up to 3 days, or in the refrigerator, covered, for 1 week.

CLASSIC SNICKERDOODLES

Rolling cookie dough in cinnamon sugar definitely sounds like it will lead to something special, and these chewy snickerdoodles are proof that it does. The cookies have crisp, chewy edges and a softer center, with enough cinnamon sugar flavor to satisfy the pickiest sweet tooth. I love them with a bowl of coconut milk ice cream for the ultimate cinnamon packed treat!

Yield: 22 cookies

COOKIES
1¼ cups (120 g) blanched almond flour

2 tbsp (16 g) coconut flour

¾ tsp cream of tartar

½ tsp baking soda

¾ tsp ground cinnamon

¼ tsp fine sea salt

6 tbsp (90 ml) melted coconut oil

6 tbsp (94 g) cashew or almond butter

⅓ cup (79 ml) pure maple syrup

2 tbsp (20 g) pure maple or coconut sugar

1 tsp pure vanilla extract

1 large egg yolk

TOPPING
3 tbsp (29 g) pure maple sugar

2 tsp (4 g) ground cinnamon

Prepare the cookies: Preheat your oven to 350°F (177°C) and line 2 large baking sheets with parchment paper.

In a medium-sized bowl, combine the almond and coconut flours, cream of tartar, baking soda, cinnamon and salt.

In a separate large bowl, use an electric mixer to cream together the coconut oil, cashew butter, maple syrup, maple sugar and vanilla until smooth. Beat in the egg yolk and mix on medium-low speed until well combined. Slowly add the dry mixture to the wet until fully combined and a dough forms (it will be soft/sticky at first). Chill the dough in the refrigerator for 20 to 30 minutes.

Once the dough is firm enough to be able to be rolled into balls, prepare the topping: In a small bowl, combine the maple sugar and cinnamon. Form the dough into 22 balls and roll each ball gently in the cinnamon sugar topping.

Place the cookie dough balls 2 inches (5 cm) apart on the prepared baking sheets and flatten each ball slightly with your hand. Bake for 8 to 10 minutes, or until the cookies appear cracked on top. They will be extremely soft but will set quickly as they cool.

Remove the cookies from the oven and allow to cool for at least 5 minutes on the baking sheets, then transfer to wire racks to cool completely.

Store the cookies, loosely covered, at room temperature for up to 4 days, or freeze to keep them longer.

GIANT FUDGY CHOCOLATE CHIP SKILLET COOKIE

We all know how comforting a fresh batch of homemade chocolate chip cookies is, but a huge chocolate chip cookie baked in a skillet? Maybe even better! This giant cookie skillet is superfudgy, chocolaty and gooey, and also happens to make a great birthday cake for cookie lovers everywhere. I love serving it with coconut milk ice cream for the ultimate chocolate chip cookie sundae.

Yield: One 10" (25-cm) skillet cookie

Coconut oil, for skillet

⅔ cup (130 g) ghee, soft

¼ cup (59 ml) pure maple syrup

⅔ cup (52 g) pure maple or coconut sugar

2 tsp (10 ml) pure vanilla extract

1 large egg

1 large egg yolk

2 cups (192 g) blanched almond flour

½ tsp baking soda

½ tsp fine sea salt

1 cup (170 g) Paleo-friendly chopped dark chocolate or dark chocolate chips

Preheat your oven to 350°F (177°C) and grease a 10-inch (25-cm) ovenproof skillet with coconut oil.

In a large bowl, using an electric hand mixer, beat together the ghee, maple syrup, maple sugar and vanilla until smooth. Add the egg and egg yolk and continue to beat until smooth. Keeping the mixer on low speed, slowly add the almond flour, baking soda and salt and mix until a sticky dough forms. Stir in the chocolate evenly, then transfer the mixture to the prepared skillet.

Bake for 22 to 25 minutes, or until deep golden brown. Remove from the oven and allow the cookie to cool for at least 20 to 30 minutes in the skillet before serving.

Store leftovers, covered, in the refrigerator for up to 5 days.

SOFT AND CHEWY GINGERBREAD COOKIES

Once the holiday season rolls around, I'm more than ready to start baking with molasses. The combination of molasses and coconut sugar used here gives these cookies a deep, sweet flavor that pairs perfectly with warm winter spices. They're pillowy soft, thick and best stored, loosely covered, at room temperature to maintain their chewy texture.

Yield: 12 to 14 cookies

1 large egg

1 large egg yolk

⅓ cup + 1 tbsp (99 g) smooth almond butter

⅓ cup + 1 tbsp (94 ml) melted refined coconut oil

⅓ cup (113 g) blackstrap molasses

¼ cup (57 g) coconut sugar, plus 2 tbsp (28 g) for sprinkling (optional)

1 tsp pure vanilla extract

⅔ cup (85 g) coconut flour

1 tsp baking soda

¼ tsp fine sea salt

1½ tsp (3 g) ground cinnamon

1½ tsp (3 g) ground ginger

¼ tsp ground allspice or cloves

Preheat your oven to 350°F (177°C) and line a large baking sheet with parchment paper.

In a large bowl, whisk or use an electric mixer to combine the egg, egg yolk, almond butter and coconut oil until smooth. Add the molasses, coconut sugar and vanilla and continue to mix until smooth.

In a separate medium-sized bowl, combine the coconut flour, baking soda, salt, cinnamon, ginger and allspice. Add the dry mixture to the wet and mix until fully combined (the dough will be sticky). Chill the dough in the freezer for 10 minutes, or until it thickens and can be easily scooped.

Use a cookie scoop or spoon to scoop the dough in heaping tablespoons (about 25 g of dough) onto the parchment paper, then gently flatten and sprinkle with coconut sugar, if desired.

Bake for 8 to 10 minutes, or until the tops crack. Don't overbake; the cookies will become firmer and chewier as they cool. Allow to cool on the baking sheet for 5 minutes, then transfer to wire racks to cool completely.

Store, loosely covered, at room temperature for the first day, then transfer to a container and refrigerate for up to 1 week.

BUTTER PECAN COOKIES

Scooping ice cream for a couple of years in high school introduced me to tons of new ice cream flavors, and butter pecan wound up being my favorite. You get a wonderful buttery flavor in these cookies from the ghee, and maple or coconut sugar adds the perfect amount of sweetness. The cookies are crisp, similar to a shortbread, and the pecans add extra crunch that makes these hard to resist.

Yield: 14 to 16 cookies

6 tbsp (90 ml) melted ghee or butter-flavored coconut oil

6 tbsp (59 g) pure maple or coconut sugar

1 tsp pure vanilla extract

1 large egg

1¾ cups (168 g) blanched almond flour

½ tsp baking soda

¼–½ tsp fine sea salt

⅔ cup (75 g) raw pecans, chopped

Preheat your oven to 350°F (177°C) and line a large baking sheet with parchment paper.

In a large bowl, whisk together the ghee, maple sugar and vanilla until smooth, then whisk in the egg.

In a separate large bowl, combine the almond flour, baking soda and salt, then stir the dry mixture into the wet until a sticky dough forms. Stir in the pecans, then, using a 1½-tablespoon (23-ml) cookie scoop, scoop balls of dough 2 inches (5 cm) apart onto the baking sheet and press down gently on each mound—these cookies won't spread on their own. Bake for 8 to 10 minutes, or until set and turning light brown.

Remove from the oven and allow the cookies to cool on the baking sheet for 5 minutes, then transfer to wire racks to cool completely.

Store the cookies, loosely covered, at room temperature for the first 2 days, then covered in the refrigerator for up to 1 week.

LEMON POPPY SEED COOKIES WITH LEMON ICING

While testing these cookies, I found the key to getting the perfect texture is chilling the dough for at least an hour. You wind up with a soft, but not too soft, chewy cookie with tons of bright lemon flavor. Add onto that a maple lemon drizzle and you'll be in lemon poppy seed heaven, I promise.

Yield: 12 to 14 cookies

COOKIES

⅓ cup (72 g) refined coconut oil, soft but solid

¼ cup (39 g) pure maple sugar

¼ cup (85 g) raw honey

1 large egg, at room temperature

½ tsp pure vanilla extract

½ tsp almond extract

½ tsp lemon extract

1 tsp fresh lemon juice

Zest of 1 medium-sized lemon

1⅔ cups (160 g) blanched almond flour

¼ cup (28 g) tapioca flour

½ tsp baking soda

¼ tsp fine sea salt

1 tbsp (8 g) poppy seeds

ICING

½ cup (78 g) powdered maple sugar (see page 12)

2–3 tsp (10–15 ml) fresh lemon juice

Prepare the cookies: In a large bowl, combine the coconut oil, maple sugar and honey. Using an electric hand mixer, beat on medium speed until creamy. Add the egg, vanilla, almond and lemon extracts, lemon juice and zest, then continue to beat on medium speed until smooth.

In a separate medium-sized bowl, combine the almond and tapioca flours, baking soda and salt. Stir the dry mixture into the wet until combined, then stir in the poppy seeds. Place the bowl in the refrigerator and chill for at least 30 minutes.

While the dough chills, preheat your oven to 350°F (177°C) and line a large baking sheet with parchment paper. After chilling, use a 1½-tablespoon (23-ml) cookie scoop to scoop the dough about 2 inches (5 cm) apart onto the prepared baking sheet. Press down just slightly in the middle of each mound. Bake for 10 minutes, or until set.

Remove from the oven and allow the cookies to cool on the baking sheet for 5 minutes, then transfer to wire racks to cool completely.

While the cookies cool, prepare the icing: In a small bowl, stir together the powdered maple sugar and the lemon juice, adding a teaspoon of juice at a time until you get the right consistency.

Drizzle the icing over the cooled cookies. The icing will harden at room temperature after 20 to 30 minutes.

Store leftovers, covered, at room temperature for the first day, then cover and refrigerate for up to 1 week.

FAVORITE QUICK BREADS *and* MUFFINS

There's something just so special and cozy about baking your favorite muffins and quick breads at home. They're simple recipes that everyone in the family loves (and can help with!)—and they make your house smell incredible while they bake!

Best of all, your favorite banana bread or blueberry muffin becomes a staple that adds a delicious moment to your day, whether it's breakfast, an afternoon coffee break or an after-dinner treat.

Many of the recipes in this chapter can be baked either in loaf form or as muffins. You'll find a mix of classics, seasonal favorites and a few that can pass as decadent desserts— that are still perfectly fine to eat for breakfast!

DOUBLE DARK CHOCOLATE ZUCCHINI MUFFINS

I was always such a skeptic about using zucchini in baking. As it turns out, zucchini can be the secret to seriously moist and tender muffins that rise beautifully in the oven—something that doesn't always come easily with Paleo baking. Add lots of dark chocolate chunks and you wind up with muffins that taste like a rich chocolate cake, yet are healthy enough to serve for breakfast.

Yield: 12 to 14 muffins

1½ cups (144 g) blanched almond flour

½ cup (50 g) raw cacao powder or unsweetened cocoa powder

1 tsp baking soda

¼ tsp fine sea salt

3 large eggs, at room temperature

½ cup (113 g) coconut sugar

¼ cup (59 ml) melted refined coconut oil, cooled to almost room temperature

¼ cup (63 g) smooth unsalted almond butter

1 tsp pure vanilla extract

2 medium-sized zucchini, peeled if desired and finely shredded, water squeezed out between paper towels (2 cups [350 g] gently packed)

¾ cup (128 g) chopped Paleo-friendly dark chocolate

Preheat your oven to 350°F (177°C) and line 12 to 14 wells of 1 or 2 muffin pans with parchment liners.

In a medium-sized bowl, combine the almond flour, cacao powder, baking soda and salt, then set aside.

In a large bowl, whisk or use an electric hand mixer to blend together the eggs, coconut sugar, coconut oil, almond butter and vanilla until well combined and smooth.

Add the dry mixture to the wet and mix until just moistened (the batter should be quite thick), then fold in the shredded zucchini, then the chocolate.

Using a spoon, fill each prepared muffin well slightly more than three-quarters of the way full. Bake for 25 minutes, or until a toothpick inserted in the center of a muffin comes out clean or with a few crumbs.

Remove from the oven and allow to cool for 10 minutes in the pan, then transfer to wire racks to cool completely.

Store the muffins at room temperature for the first day, then covered in the refrigerator for up to 5 days.

Note: These muffins can also be baked as a loaf. Line an 8½ x 4½–inch (22 x 11–cm) loaf pan with parchment paper. Spread the batter evenly in the pan and bake at 350°F (177°C) for 45 to 55 minutes, or until a toothpick inserted into the center comes out clean or with a few crumbs.

SPICED HONEY APPLE ALMOND MUFFINS

Honey and warm spices make just about everything better! These simple, sweet, moist and tender muffins have double the apples and a nutty flavor thanks to almond butter, almond flour and crunchy sliced almonds.

Yield: 12 to 14 muffins

---

3 large eggs

⅓ cup (83 g) smooth almond butter

2 medium-sized apples, one peeled and grated, excess water squeezed out (about ⅔ cup [80 g] grated apple); the other peeled and finely diced (about 1 cup [120 g])

⅓ cup (113 g) raw honey

2 tbsp (30 ml) fresh lemon juice

3 tbsp (45 ml) melted refined coconut oil, cooled

1 tsp pure vanilla extract

2 cups (192 g) blanched almond flour

¾ tsp baking soda

½ tsp fine sea salt

1 tbsp (6 g) apple pie spice (see Notes)

2 tsp (4 g) ground cinnamon

½ cup (43 g) sliced almonds

Preheat your oven to 350°F (177°C) and line 12 to 14 wells of 1 or 2 muffin pans with parchment liners.

In a large bowl, whisk or use an electric hand mixer to blend together the eggs, almond butter, grated apple, honey, lemon juice, coconut oil and vanilla.

In a separate large bowl, combine the almond flour, baking soda, salt, apple pie spice and cinnamon. Stir the dry mixture into the wet with a spoon until just combined. Fold in the diced apple.

Using a spoon, fill each prepared muffin well just over three-quarters full. Arrange the sliced almonds on top. Bake for 20 minutes, or until a toothpick inserted in the center of a muffin comes out clean.

Remove from the oven and allow the muffins to cool in the pan for 5 to 10 minutes, then transfer to wire racks to cool completely.

Store the muffins, loosely covered, at room temperature for the first day, then cover and refrigerate for up to 5 days.

Notes: You can also make your own apple pie spice. Combine 1½ tablespoons (9 g) of ground cinnamon, 1½ teaspoons (3 g) of ground nutmeg and 1 teaspoon of ground allspice. Use just 1 tablespoon (6 g) of this mixture for this recipe and save the rest for another use.

These muffins can also be baked as a loaf: Line an 8½ x 4½–inch (22 x 11–cm) loaf pan with parchment paper. Spread the batter evenly in the pan and bake at 350°F (177°C) for 45 minutes, or until golden brown and a toothpick inserted near the center of the loaf comes out clean or with a few crumbs.

BLUEBERRY ALMOND BUTTER BANANA BREAD

This bread brings together two combos that I can't get enough of: banana–almond butter and banana-blueberry! The almond butter gives the bread a nutty flavor and fluffy texture that makes it irresistible and totally comforting, too. It's perfect for after-school snacks, quick breakfasts or even a healthy dessert.

Yield: 1 medium-sized loaf (10 servings)

---

3 overripe bananas

3 large eggs

½ cup (125 g) smooth almond butter, no sugar or salt added

⅓ cup (75 g) coconut sugar or maple sugar

1 tsp pure vanilla extract

1 tbsp (15 ml) fresh lemon juice

1¾ cups (168 g) blanched almond flour

¼ cup (28 g) tapioca flour

2 tsp (4 g) ground cinnamon

1 tsp baking soda

½ tsp fine sea salt

1 cup (170 g) blueberries

Preheat your oven to 350°F (177°C) and line an 8½ x 4½–inch (22 x 11–cm) loaf pan with parchment paper, allowing two opposite ends of the paper to overhang for easy lifting.

In a large bowl, mash the bananas well, then whisk in the eggs, almond butter, coconut sugar, vanilla and lemon juice.

In a separate bowl, combine the almond and tapioca flours, cinnamon, baking soda and salt. Stir the dry mixture into the wet until fully combined, then fold in three-quarters of the blueberries.

Transfer to the prepared loaf pan, sprinkle the remaining blueberries on top and gently swirl them in. Bake for 44 to 55 minutes, or until a toothpick inserted near the center of the loaf comes out clean and the top is deep golden brown.

Remove from the oven and allow the loaf to cool in the pan on a wire rack for 20 minutes. Then remove using the parchment paper to help you, and continue to cool on the wire rack to room temperature before slicing.

Store the loaf, loosely covered, at room temperature for the first day, then cover and refrigerate for up to 5 days.

Note: This loaf can also be baked as muffins: Transfer the batter to a parchment-lined 12-well muffin pan, filling the wells three-quarters full. Bake at 350°F (177°C) for 22 to 25 minutes, or until the muffins rise and appear golden brown. Remove from the oven and allow them to cool in the pan for 10 minutes, then transfer to wire racks to cool completely before serving.

CHOCOLATE CHUNK TAHINI BANANA MUFFINS

It's hard to say no to big chunks of dark chocolate when it comes to, well, basically anything, and these moist and tender banana muffins are no exception! The dark chocolate and tahini give these banana muffins a richer flavor and texture than most in the best way possible.

Yield: 12 muffins

3 large eggs

2 overripe medium-sized bananas, mashed (about 1 cup [300 g])

½ cup (125 g) sesame tahini

⅓ cup (79 ml) pure maple syrup

2 tsp (10 ml) pure vanilla extract

1¼ cups (120 g) blanched almond flour

⅓ cup (55 g) flaxseed meal

1 tsp ground cinnamon

1 tsp baking soda

¼ tsp fine sea salt

1 cup (170 g) roughly chopped Paleo-friendly dark chocolate

Preheat your oven to 350°F (177°C) and line a 12-well muffin pan with parchment liners.

In a large bowl, whisk together the eggs, mashed bananas, tahini, maple syrup and vanilla.

In a separate bowl, combine the almond flour, flaxseed meal, cinnamon, baking soda and salt. Stir the dry mixture into the wet until just combined, then fold in the dark chocolate.

Using a spoon, fill each prepared muffin well just over three-quarters full. Bake for 20 minutes, or until a toothpick inserted in the center of a muffin comes out clean.

Remove from the oven and allow the muffins to cool in the pan for 5 to 10 minutes, then transfer to wire racks to cool completely.

Store the muffins, loosely covered, at room temperature for the first day, then cover and refrigerate for up to 5 days.

Note: These muffins can also be baked as a loaf: Line an 8½ x 4½–inch (22 x 11–cm) loaf pan with parchment paper. Spread the batter evenly in the pan and bake at 350°F (177°C) for 45 to 55 minutes.

CINNAMON RAISIN BANANA BREAD (NO SUGAR ADDED)

Superripe bananas and juicy raisins give this bread all the sweetness it needs. It's perfect toasted and slathered with almond butter or enjoyed on its own. Trust me—it won't last long in your house!

Yield: 1 medium-sized loaf (10 servings)

2 cups (192 g) blanched almond flour

½ cup (56 g) tapioca flour

1 tsp baking soda

1 tbsp (6 g) ground cinnamon

½ tsp fine sea salt

3 very overripe medium-sized bananas, mashed (about 1¼ cups [375 g])

4 large eggs, at room temperature

1 tbsp (15 ml) fresh lemon juice

2 tsp (10 ml) pure vanilla extract

2 tbsp (30 ml) melted coconut oil, cooled to almost room temperature

¾ cup (113 g) raisins

Preheat your oven to 350°F (177°C) and line an 8½ x 4½–inch (22 x 11–cm) loaf pan with parchment paper, allowing two opposite ends of the paper to overhang for easy lifting.

In a large bowl, whisk together the almond and tapioca flours, baking soda, cinnamon and salt.

In a separate large bowl, whisk together the mashed bananas, eggs, lemon juice, vanilla and coconut oil until well combined. Slowly stir the dry mixture into the wet, using a spoon or rubber spatula, just until moistened and no visible flour remains, then fold in the raisins.

Transfer the batter to the prepared loaf pan and bake for 50 minutes, or until deep golden brown and a toothpick inserted into the center of the loaf comes out clean.

Remove from the oven and allow the loaf to cool completely in the pan on a wire rack, then remove, using the parchment paper to help you. Slice and serve.

Store leftovers, loosely covered, at room temperature for the first day, then cover and store in the refrigerator for up to 4 days. You can gently reheat in a toaster oven, if desired.

Note: This loaf can also be baked as muffins: Transfer the batter to a parchment-lined 12-well muffin pan, filling the wells three-quarters full. Bake at 350°F (177°C) for 22 to 25 minutes, or until the muffins rise and appear golden brown. Remove from the oven and allow the muffins to cool in the pan for 10 minutes, then transfer to wire racks to cool completely before serving.

APPLE CINNAMON BREAD
WITH WALNUT STREUSEL

This loaf has it all—a double dose of juicy sweet apples, warm spices, a crunchy nutty streusel topping and a drizzle of maple icing. Whether it's breakfast, a snack or dessert, this cozy apple cinnamon bread is a favorite.

Yield: 1 medium-sized loaf (10 servings)

STREUSEL

¼ cup (24 g) blanched almond flour

2 tbsp (28 g) coconut oil, solid

3 tbsp (42 g) coconut sugar

1½ tsp (3 g) ground cinnamon

Large pinch of sea salt

¼ cup (28 g) chopped walnuts

BREAD

1 cup (96 g) blanched almond flour

¼ cup (32 g) coconut flour

⅓ cup (37 g) tapioca flour

1 tbsp (6 g) ground cinnamon

¼ tsp fine sea salt

1 tsp baking soda

4 large eggs

¼ cup (59 ml) unsweetened almond milk

1½ tsp (8 ml) pure vanilla extract

6 tbsp (84 g) coconut sugar

BREAD (CONT.)

2 medium-sized apples, one peeled and grated, excess water squeezed out (about ⅔ cup [80 g] measured after squeezing); the other peeled and finely diced (about 1 cup [120 g])

3 tbsp (45 ml) melted coconut oil, cooled

1 tbsp (15 ml) fresh lemon juice

⅓ cup (38 g) chopped walnuts

ICING

½ cup (78 g) powdered pure maple or coconut sugar (see page 12)

2–3 tsp (10–15 ml) unsweetened almond milk

Preheat your oven to 350°F (177°C) and line an 8½ x 4½–inch (22 x 11–cm) loaf pan with parchment paper, allowing two opposite ends of the paper to overhang for easy lifting.

Prepare the streusel: In a medium bowl, using a fork, combine all the streusel ingredients, except the walnuts, until well mixed (it should look like crumbs). Stir in the walnuts, then chill in the fridge while you prepare the batter.

Prepare the bread: In a medium-sized bowl, combine the almond, coconut and tapioca flours, plus the cinnamon, salt and baking soda.

In a large bowl, whisk together the eggs, almond milk, vanilla, coconut sugar, grated apple, coconut oil and lemon juice until well combined. Gently stir the dry mixture into the wet until no flour spots show, then fold in the diced apple and chopped walnuts.

Transfer to the prepared baking pan and spread evenly. Sprinkle all the streusel over the top, then bake for 45 to 50 minutes, or until a toothpick inserted near the center of the loaf comes out clean.

(continued)

APPLE CINNAMON BREAD
WITH WALNUT STREUSEL (CONT.)

Remove from the oven and allow the loaf to cool in the pan on a wire rack for about 20 minutes, then remove, using the parchment paper overhang to help you, and continue to cool on the wire rack.

While the loaf cools, prepare the icing: In a small bowl, stir together the maple sugar and almond milk until you get the consistency of a drizzly icing.

Cool the bread on a wire rack, then drizzle the icing all over the top of the loaf and allow to cool for another 10 minutes before serving.

Note: This loaf can also be baked as muffins: Transfer the batter to a parchment-lined 12-well muffin pan, filling the wells three-quarters full, then sprinkle the chilled streusel over the muffins. Bake at 350°F (177°C) for 22 to 25 minutes, or until a toothpick inserted in the center of a muffin comes out clean or with a few crumbs.

PUMPKIN STREUSEL BREAD

No matter what the season, I can't resist the warm pumpkin pie spices that make this loaf the ultimate comforting quick bread. Classic moist, tender pumpkin bread is topped with loads of sweet streusel plus a drizzle that's reminiscent of brown sugar. I like storing this bread in the refrigerator after the first day and warming it just slightly in the toaster.

Yield: 1 medium-sized loaf (10 servings)

BREAD

3 large eggs

1 cup (225 g) organic pumpkin puree

¼ cup (59 ml) melted organic refined coconut oil

¼ cup (57 g) coconut sugar

¼ cup (85 g) raw honey

1 tsp pure vanilla extract

2 cups (192 g) blanched almond flour

6 tbsp (42 g) tapioca or arrowroot flour

1 tsp baking soda

1 tbsp (6 g) pumpkin pie spice

1 tsp ground cinnamon

¼ tsp fine sea salt

STREUSEL

½ cup (48 g) blanched almond flour

⅓ cup (75 g) coconut sugar

1 tsp pumpkin pie spice

⅛ tsp fine sea salt

¼ cup (49 g) ghee, solid, or coconut oil

Prepare the bread: Preheat your oven to 350°F (177°C) and line an 8½ x 4½–inch (22 x 11–cm) loaf pan with parchment paper, allowing two opposite ends of the paper to overhang for easy lifting.

In a large bowl, whisk together the eggs, pumpkin puree, coconut oil, coconut sugar, honey and vanilla.

In a separate bowl, combine the almond and tapioca flours, baking soda, pumpkin pie spice, cinnamon and salt, then stir the dry mixture into the wet until just combined. Transfer the batter to the prepared loaf pan.

Prepare the streusel: In a small bowl, combine all the streusel ingredients, using a pastry blender or fork, until thick crumbs form. Sprinkle the streusel all over the top of the loaf to cover it.

Bake the loaf for 55 minutes, covering it with aluminum foil after 30 minutes to avoid excessive browning, if necessary. A toothpick inserted near the center of the loaf should come out clean or with a few crumbs.

Remove from the oven and allow the loaf to cool in the pan for 30 minutes, then remove, using the parchment paper to help you, and transfer to a wire rack to cool completely.

(continued)

PUMPKIN STREUSEL BREAD (CONT.)

ICING

½ cup (113 g) powdered maple or coconut sugar (see page 12)

2–3 tsp (10–15 ml) almond or coconut milk

¼ tsp pure vanilla extract

Once the bread has cooled, prepare the icing: In a small bowl, whisk together the icing ingredients and drizzle it all over the bread. Let sit for 20 minutes so the icing can harden, then slice and serve.

Store leftovers, covered, in the refrigerator for up to 5 days.

Note: This loaf can also be baked as muffins: Transfer the batter to a parchment-lined 12-well muffin pan, filling the wells three-quarters full, then sprinkle the chilled streusel over the muffins. Bake at 350°F (177°C) for 22 to 25 minutes, or until a toothpick inserted in the center of a muffin comes out clean or with a few crumbs.

DOUBLE CHOCOLATE CHIP ESPRESSO MUFFINS

I'm never one to turn down chocolate in any form, especially when coffee is involved, too. The espresso powder in these muffins gives the chocolate extra depth and richness, and the almond butter gives them a superior texture and rise. I recommend storing these at room temperature to keep the perfectly crisp muffin top texture that makes these special.

Yield: 12 to 14 muffins

1⅓ cups (128 g) blanched almond flour

6 tbsp (38 g) raw cacao powder

2 tbsp (14 g) pure espresso powder

1 tsp baking soda

¼ tsp fine sea salt

3 large eggs

½ cup (125 g) smooth almond butter

½ cup (119 ml) pure maple syrup

⅓ cup (79 ml) melted coconut oil, cooled

1 tsp pure vanilla extract

1 cup (170 g) Paleo-friendly dark chocolate chips

Preheat your oven to 350°F (177°C) and line 12 to 14 wells of 1 or 2 muffin pans with parchment liners.

In a medium-sized bowl, combine the almond flour, cacao powder, espresso powder, baking soda and salt.

In a large bowl, whisk or use an electric hand mixer to blend together the eggs, almond butter, maple syrup, coconut oil and vanilla until well combined and smooth. Add the dry mixture to the wet until just moistened, then stir in the chocolate.

Using a spoon, fill each prepared muffin well just over three-quarters full. Bake for 18 to 22 minutes, or until a toothpick inserted in the center of a muffin comes out with a few crumbs.

Remove from the oven and allow the muffins to cool for 10 minutes in the pan, then transfer to wire racks to cool completely.

Store, loosely covered, at room temperature for the first day, then cover and refrigerate for up to 1 week.

Note: These muffins can also be baked as a loaf: Line an 8½ x 4½–inch (22 x 11–cm) loaf pan with parchment paper. Spread the batter evenly in the pan and bake at 350°F (177°C) for 45 to 50 minutes, or until a toothpick inserted near the center of the loaf comes out clean or with a few crumbs. Cool in the pan on a wire rack for 20 minutes, then transfer to a wire rack to cool completely before slicing and serving.

LEMON BLUEBERRY MUFFINS

I absolutely love baking with fresh lemons, not only for the incredible flavor, but also for the texture it brings to Paleo baking! Lemon interacts with the baking soda in breads, muffins and cakes, helping them rise more like traditional quick breads. The combination of blanched almond flour and tapioca flour I use also helps mimic the texture of traditional wheat flour muffins. These sweet, tart muffins with juicy blueberries are equally perfect to grab for breakfast, serve to company for brunch or make ahead for after-school snacks.

Yield: 12 muffins

---

2 cups (192 g) blanched almond flour

½ cup (56 g) tapioca flour

1 tsp baking soda

½ tsp ground cinnamon

¼ tsp fine sea salt

4 large eggs

¼ cup (85 g) raw honey

¼ cup (50 g) pure maple sugar or coconut sugar

⅓ cup (79 ml) fresh lemon juice (from 2–3 lemons)

Zest of 1 medium-sized lemon

¼ cup (59 ml) melted coconut oil, cooled to almost room temperature

1 tsp pure vanilla extract

½ tsp pure almond extract

1 cup (170 g) blueberries

Preheat your oven to 350°F (177°C) and line a 12-well muffin pan with parchment liners.

In a medium-sized bowl, stir together the almond and tapioca flours, baking soda, cinnamon and salt.

In a large bowl, whisk or use an electric hand mixer to blend together the eggs, honey, maple sugar, lemon juice and zest, coconut oil, vanilla and almond extract until smooth. Stir the dry mixture into the wet until fully combined, then fold in the blueberries.

Fill the prepared muffin cups just over three-quarters of the way. Bake for 15 to 17 minutes, or until a toothpick inserted in the center of a muffin comes out clean.

Remove from the oven and allow the muffins to cool in the pan for 10 minutes, then transfer to wire racks to cool completely.

Store the muffins, loosely covered, at room temperature for the first day and covered in the refrigerator after that.

Note: These muffins can also be baked as a loaf: Line an 8½ x 4½–inch (22 x 11–cm) loaf pan with parchment paper. Spread the batter evenly in the pan and bake at 350°F (177°C) for 45 to 55 minutes, or until deep golden brown and a toothpick inserted near the center of the loaf comes out with a few crumbs. Cool in the pan on a wire rack for 20 minutes, then remove from the pan using the parchment paper and continue to cool completely on the rack before slicing and serving.

CHOCOLATE CHIP MINI MUFFINS

When I was a kid, there was pretty much nothing better than a bag of those Little Bites mini muffins. Moist, sweet and oh so snack-able, this healthier homemade version of the classic chocolate chip mini muffins is bound to become a family favorite. I love them with extra mini chocolate chips sprinkled on top of each muffin right before baking.

Yield: 24 mini muffins

Coconut oil spray (optional)

1¾ cups (168 g) blanched almond flour

⅓ cup (37 g) tapioca flour

¾ tsp baking soda

¼ tsp fine sea salt

3 large eggs

¼ cup (59 ml) canned full-fat coconut milk, blended prior to adding

⅓ cup (113 g) raw honey

2 tbsp (30 ml) melted ghee

1 tsp pure vanilla extract

1½ tsp (8 ml) fresh lemon juice

¾ cup (128 g) Paleo-friendly mini chocolate chips or chopped dark chocolate

Preheat your oven to 350°F (177°C) and line a 24-well mini muffin pan with parchment liners (see Note) or spray the wells with coconut oil spray.

In a medium-sized bowl, combine the almond and tapioca flours, baking soda and salt.

In a separate large bowl, whisk or use an electric hand mixer to blend together the eggs, coconut milk, honey, ghee, vanilla and lemon juice. Stir the dry mixture into the wet until fully combined, then stir in the chocolate.

Using a spoon, fill the prepared muffin cups about three-quarters full. Bake for 12 to 14 minutes, or until golden brown and a toothpick inserted in the center of a muffin comes out clean.

Remove from the oven and allow to cool in the pan for 10 minutes, then transfer to wire racks to cool completely.

Store the muffins, loosely covered, at room temperature for the first day, then covered in the refrigerator for up to 5 days.

Note: I buy my mini parchment liners from the brand PaperChef, available from Amazon. If you can't find mini parchment liners, make sure you use a good nonstick pan and spray well with coconut oil spray.

HONEY "CORN" MUFFINS

Trying to mimic the flavor of cornbread without corn is not an easy task at all. However, this combination of ghee, coconut milk, honey and almond and coconut flours does as close of a job as I can imagine with a flavor and texture reminiscent of traditional corn muffins. These sweet "corn" muffins are perfect with breakfast and can be eaten warm out of the oven or toasted. Plus, they come together quickly and easily.

Yield: 12 muffins

4 large eggs, at room temperature

½ cup (119 ml) full-fat coconut milk, at room temperature or slightly warmed, blended prior to adding

1 tbsp (15 ml) fresh lemon juice

6 tbsp (128 g) raw honey

¼ cup (59 ml) melted ghee

1¾ cups (168 g) blanched almond flour

¼ cup (32 g) coconut flour

1½ tsp (3 g) aluminum-free baking powder or homemade Paleo baking powder (see page 12)

½ tsp baking soda

½ tsp fine sea salt

Preheat your oven to 325°F (163°C) and line a 12-well muffin pan with parchment liners.

In a large bowl, whisk or use an electric mixer to blend together the eggs, coconut milk, lemon juice, honey and ghee until smooth.

In a separate medium-sized bowl, combine the almond and coconut flours, baking powder, baking soda and salt. Add the dry mixture to the wet and mix until just combined.

Using a spoon, fill each prepared muffin well a bit more than three-quarters of the way. Bake for 22 minutes, or until golden brown and a toothpick inserted in the center of a muffin comes out clean.

Remove from the oven and allow to cool in the pan for 10 minutes, then transfer to wire racks to cool almost completely. These muffins are best served slightly warm.

Store leftovers, loosely covered, at room temperature for the first day, then covered in the refrigerator for up to 4 days.

RICH *and* CHEWY BROWNIES *and* BARS

This chapter is probably the most varied in the book—we have everything from gooey Salted Caramel Turtle Brownies (page 111) to Creamy Lemon Bars (page 103) to Cherry Pie Bars (page 104) to Vanilla Frosted Sugar Cookie Bars (page 116) and beyond. Some bars are fruity, some fudgy and one is even stuffed with cookie dough—so you know there's a lot to look forward to!

Most of these brownies and bars come together quickly but need several hours to cool before you can actually dig in. In fact, most will also need some time in the refrigerator for the very best texture. Believe me, I know it's hard to wait! However, you'll be well rewarded when you take a bite of that first square. These clean-eating treats are easy to share and easy to love.

TRIPLE CHOCOLATE FUDGE BROWNIES

Brownies are one dessert that everyone can get excited about, don't you think?
Seriously, chocolate actually *does* win every time, and the more the better when it comes
to brownies! Raw cacao, melted chocolate and chocolate chunks make these extra
chocolaty with rich flavor and a chewy, fudgelike texture. They're family approved
and perfect when you need a healthier chocolate indulgence.

Yield: 16 brownies

½ cup (48 g) blanched almond flour

¼ cup (25 g) raw cacao powder

¼ tsp baking soda

¼ tsp fine sea salt

4 oz (113 g) unsweetened baking chocolate, cut into small pieces

⅓ cup (83 g) unsalted almond butter

⅓ cup (72 g) refined coconut oil

¼ cup (59 ml) pure maple syrup

⅔ cup (151 g) coconut sugar

1 tsp pure vanilla extract

2 large eggs

⅓ cup (57 g) chopped Paleo-friendly dark chocolate or dark chocolate chips

Preheat your oven to 350°F (177°C) and line an 8-inch (20-cm) square pan with parchment paper on the bottom and up the sides.

In a medium-sized bowl, stir together the almond flour, cacao powder, baking soda and salt and set aside.

In a microwave-safe glass bowl, combine the unsweetened chocolate and almond butter and microwave in increments of 30 seconds, stirring after each increment until smooth.

Add the coconut oil to the chocolate mixture and stir until smooth and melted, then add the maple syrup, coconut sugar and vanilla. Whisk in the eggs, 1 at a time, until smooth and combined. Stir in the dry mixture, then fold in the chopped dark chocolate.

Transfer the mixture to the prepared pan and bake for 16 to 18 minutes, or until just set in the center.

Remove from the oven and allow the brownies to cool completely to room temperature in their pan before cutting into squares (see Note).

Store leftovers, covered, in the refrigerator for up to 5 days.

Note: For cleaner edges and a fudgier texture when cutting them into squares, refrigerate the brownies for 2 hours prior to cutting. This is optional, but recommended for optimal texture.

CREAMY LEMON BARS

Getting the texture right for both the crust and the filling for these lemon bars was a bit of a challenge. I wanted a chewy, sweet cookie crust and a creamy, tart-yet-sweet lemon layer, and it didn't come easily! After several tries, I came up with a recipe very close to traditional lemon bars that will become a sure favorite for lemon lovers everywhere!

Yield: 12 to 16 bars

CRUST
¼ cup (49 g) ghee

⅓ cup (52 g) pure maple sugar

1 tsp pure vanilla extract

1½ cups (144 g) blanched almond flour

¼ cup (28 g) tapioca flour

¼ tsp fine sea salt

Zest of 1 lemon

1 large egg

LEMON LAYER
⅔ cup (158 ml) fresh lemon juice (from about 5 lemons)

Zest of 1 lemon

½ cup (170 g) raw honey

3 large eggs

1 large egg yolk

3 tbsp (21 g) tapioca or arrowroot flour

OPTIONAL TOPPING
Lemon zest and/or organic powdered sugar (see page 12)

Prepare the crust: In a large bowl, using an electric hand mixer, cream together the ghee, maple sugar and vanilla. With the mixer on low speed, add the almond and tapioca flours, salt, lemon zest and egg and mix until a sticky dough forms. Chill the dough in the refrigerator for 10 minutes.

Preheat your oven to 325°F (163°C). Line an 8-inch (20-cm) square pan with parchment paper on the bottom and up the sides.

Press the chilled dough evenly into the bottom of the prepared pan, then bake for 15 minutes.

While the crust bakes, make the lemon layer: In a medium-sized bowl, using an electric hand mixer, combine the lemon juice, zest and honey on low speed. Whisk in the eggs, 1 at a time, then the egg yolk. Keeping the mixer on low speed, add the tapioca flour, then mix until very smooth.

After the crust has baked, remove it from the oven and pour the filling mixture over the hot crust (do not allow the crust to cool first), then return the pan to the oven to bake for another 18 to 20 minutes, or until the center of the filling is just set and no longer jiggly. The top may crack a bit; this is normal and won't affect the texture of the bars.

Remove from the oven and allow to cool completely on a wire rack. I also recommend refrigerating the pan for an hour to make cutting easier. Cut into 12 to 16 bars. Top with some extra grated lemon zest, or dust with organic powdered sugar, if preferred.

Store leftovers, covered, in the refrigerator for up to 1 week.

Note: Oddly, the crust and filling can actually combine while baking if you wait too long to pour the filling over the partially baked crust. The key is to pour the filling over the hot crust right after the crust is finished baking—the eggs will start cooking immediately, creating a nice separation between the chewy crust and the creamy, sweet-tart filling.

CHERRY PIE BARS

Okay, so I didn't make a cherry pie for this book, *but* you're getting a recipe that might even be better—and it's easier to make than a pie! These cherry pie bars have a pastry crust that doubles as a topping, a gooey sweet cherry filling and a maple glaze that's seriously addicting.

Yield: 16 bars

CRUST AND TOPPING

1½ cups (144 g) blanched almond flour

1 cup (112 g) tapioca flour

⅓ cup (52 g) pure maple or coconut sugar

⅔ cup (130 g) ghee, palm oil shortening or grass-fed butter, cold, broken or cut into pieces

1 tsp pure vanilla extract

1 tsp pure almond extract

½ tsp fine sea salt

2 large eggs

CHERRY FILLING

2½ cups (563 g) pitted fresh or frozen cherries (no need to thaw)

¼ cup (39 g) pure maple or coconut sugar

2 tbsp (30 ml) fresh lemon juice

1 tbsp (7 g) tapioca flour

Pinch of fine sea salt

¼ tsp pure vanilla extract

OPTIONAL MAPLE GLAZE

½ cup (78 g) powdered maple sugar (see page 12)

2–3 tsp (10–15 ml) unsweetened almond milk

½ tsp pure vanilla extract

Prepare the crust and topping: You can use a food processor for this, or a pastry blender or fork. In a food processor or a large bowl, combine the almond and tapioca flours, maple sugar, ghee, vanilla, almond extract and salt and blend until coarse crumbs form. Pulse or stir in the eggs to form a sticky dough. Gather the dough into a ball, place it back in the bowl, cover and chill in the refrigerator for 30 minutes.

Meanwhile, prepare the filling: In a large saucepan, combine the cherries, maple sugar, lemon juice, tapioca flour and salt and place over medium heat. Bring to a boil, stirring, then lower the heat and allow the mixture to simmer until thickened, 2 to 5 minutes. Remove from the heat and stir in the vanilla, then set aside to cool and continue to thicken.

Preheat your oven to 350°F (177°C). Line an 8- or 9-inch (20- or 23-cm) square pan with parchment paper.

Spread half of the chilled dough on the bottom of the prepared pan and bake for 12 minutes. Chill the remaining dough while the bottom crust bakes.

When the 12 minutes are up, remove the pan from the oven and top the warm crust with the partially cooled cherry filling, then crumble the remaining chilled dough over the top.

Return the pan to the oven to bake for 30 to 35 additional minutes, or until browned on top and bubbling. Remove from the oven and allow to cool completely before cutting into bars.

For the optional glaze: Whisk together the powdered maple sugar, almond milk and vanilla extract until smooth and drizzle all over the bars. Store leftovers in the refrigerator for up to 5 days.

SALTED CARAMEL COOKIE CRUMBLE BARS

I love making cookie bars and had to include more than one in this book! The rich salted caramel for this recipe can be used for anything—topping ice cream, dipping fruit and even adding to coffee. Although these bars have three layers—the cookie, the caramel and the topping—the crust and topping are the same mixture, making them easy to throw together.

Yield: 12 to 16 bars

SALTED CARAMEL

1 (14-oz [403-ml]) can full-fat coconut milk, blended prior to adding

⅓ cup (75 g) coconut sugar

1 tsp pure vanilla extract

¼–½ tsp fine sea salt

CRUST AND TOPPING

½ cup (98 g) ghee

⅔ cup (151 g) coconut sugar

1 tsp pure vanilla extract

1 large egg, at room temperature

2 cups (192 g) blanched almond flour

¼ cup (28 g) tapioca flour

½ tsp baking soda

¼–½ tsp fine sea salt

⅓ cup (38 g) chopped pecans (optional)

Prepare the caramel first: In a medium-sized saucepan, combine the coconut milk and coconut sugar over medium heat and stir. Bring to a boil, stirring occasionally to make sure the sugar doesn't burn.

Once the mixture is boiling, lower the heat to medium-low so the mixture continues to bubble but doesn't overflow. Continue to cook, stirring occasionally, for another 25 minutes, or until reduced to 1 cup (237 ml), thickened and caramel color. Remove from the heat and stir in the vanilla and salt. Set aside to cool until you're ready to use.

Prepare the crust and topping: Preheat your oven to 350°F (177°C) and line an 8-inch (20-cm) square pan with parchment paper on the bottom and up the sides.

In a large bowl, using an electric hand mixer, beat together the ghee, coconut sugar, vanilla and egg.

In a separate medium-sized bowl, combine the almond and tapioca flours, baking soda and salt. Stir the dry mixture into the wet until a dough forms. Chill the dough in the refrigerator for 15 minutes, then press two-thirds of it into the bottom of the prepared baking pan. Bake for 10 to 12 minutes, or until set and turning golden brown.

Remove the pan from the oven, pour ¾ cup (178 ml) of the cooled caramel over the crust, then sprinkle half of the chopped pecans over the top, if using. Drop small pieces of the remaining dough over the pecans and then top with the remaining pecans.

Bake for another 15 to 18 minutes, or until the cookie topping is set and the caramel is bubbling.

Remove from the oven and allow the pan to cool completely to room temperature before cutting into squares. You can place the pan in the refrigerator to speed up the cooling time. Drizzle the remaining caramel sauce over the bars, or save it for another use. Store leftovers, covered, in the refrigerator for up to 5 days.

PEACH STREUSEL BARS

I made these cinnamon-spiced bars on a whim after loving the Cherry Pie Bars (page 104).
With a juicy, sweet, gooey peach filling, a pecan-cookie streusel topping and maple icing,
these bars are bound to disappear fast when you serve them!

Yield: 16 bars

CRUST AND TOPPING
1¾ cups (168 g) blanched almond flour

½ cup (56 g) tapioca flour

½ cup (113 g) coconut sugar

½ cup (98 g) ghee or grass-fed butter, solid

1 tsp pure vanilla extract

1 tsp ground cinnamon

½ tsp sea salt

1 large egg

½ cup (57 g) chopped pecans

PEACH FILLING
3 cups (675 g) peeled and diced fresh or frozen peaches (no need to thaw if frozen)

2 tbsp (20 g) pure maple or coconut sugar

2 tbsp (30 ml) fresh lemon juice

2 tsp (5 g) tapioca flour

Pinch of sea salt

¼ tsp pure vanilla extract

GLAZE
½ cup (78 g) powdered maple sugar (see page 12)

2–3 tsp (10–15 ml) unsweetened almond milk

½ tsp pure vanilla extract

Prepare the crust and topping: You can use a food processor for this, or a pastry blender or fork. In a food processor or a large bowl, combine the almond and tapioca flours, coconut sugar, ghee, vanilla, cinnamon and salt and blend until coarse crumbs form. Pulse or stir in the egg to form a sticky dough. Gather the dough into a ball and chill in the bowl for 30 minutes.

Meanwhile, prepare the peach filling: In a large saucepan, combine the peaches, maple sugar, lemon juice, tapioca flour and salt and place over medium heat. Bring to a boil, stirring, then lower the heat and allow the mixture to simmer until thickened, about 2 minutes. Remove from the heat and stir in the vanilla, then set aside to cool and continue to thicken.

Preheat your oven to 350°F (177°C) and line an 8- or 9-inch (20- or 23-cm) square pan with parchment paper.

Spread half of the chilled dough on the bottom of the prepared pan. Bake for 10 to 12 minutes, or until set in the center.

In a small bowl, mix the chopped pecans with the remaining dough and chill. Once the crust has baked, spread the peach filling over it and sprinkle the chilled dough mixture all over the top. Return the pan to the oven to bake for 30 to 35 additional minutes, or until browned on top and bubbling.

Remove from the oven and allow to cool completely in the pan.

Once cooled, prepare the glaze: In a small bowl, stir together the glaze ingredients until you get the right consistency for drizzling. Drizzle all over the cooled streusel and allow the pan to sit for 20 more minutes before cutting into squares. Chilling the pan will make it easier to cut.

You can sub in lemon or orange juice for the almond milk in the icing for a citrusy glaze, if you'd like.

SALTED CARAMEL TURTLE BROWNIES

When I learned how to make Paleo-friendly salted caramel with just a few simple ingredients, I went completely wild and made salted caramel everything. But I never actually tried pouring the caramel over rich chocolate fudge brownies and topping them with pecans—so, obviously I had to make it happen for this book! Gooey and crazy addicting, these turtle brownies are best stored in the refrigerator to keep their texture.

Yield: 16 brownies

SALTED CARAMEL

1 cup (237 ml) canned full-fat coconut milk, blended prior to adding

¼ cup (57 g) coconut sugar

1 tsp pure vanilla extract

¼ tsp fine sea salt

BROWNIES

⅔ cup (144 g) refined coconut oil

2 oz (57 g) unsweetened baking chocolate, chopped

1 cup (226 g) coconut sugar

2 large eggs, at room temperature

1 large egg yolk, at room temperature

1 tsp pure vanilla extract

¼ cup (25 g) raw cacao powder

½ cup (48 g) blanched almond flour

¼ tsp baking soda

¼ tsp fine sea salt

1 cup (113 g) chopped pecans, divided

½ cup (85 g) chopped Paleo-friendly dark chocolate

Prepare the caramel: In a saucepan, combine the coconut milk and coconut sugar and place over medium heat. Whisking, bring to a boil. Once boiling, continue to cook over medium heat, making sure you continue to whisk to prevent burning, for 15 to 20 minutes, or until the mixture is reduced, thickened and a deep caramel color. Remove from the heat and stir in the vanilla and salt. Set aside to cool completely.

Meanwhile, prepare the brownies: Preheat your oven to 350°F (177°C) and line an 8-inch (20-cm) square pan with parchment paper on the bottom and up the sides.

In a microwave-safe bowl, combine the coconut oil and unsweetened chocolate. Melt in the microwave in 30-second increments, whisking after each increment, until completely smooth. Whisk in the coconut sugar until completely combined, then the eggs, egg yolk and vanilla. Add the cacao powder, almond flour, baking soda, salt, half of the pecans and all of the dark chocolate.

Mix everything to fully combine, then transfer the batter to the prepared pan. Bake for 20 minutes, or until just set.

Remove from the oven and pour the cooled caramel over the top, starting in the center and spreading outward, avoiding the edges. Sprinkle the remaining pecans over the top.

Allow the brownies to cool in the pan for 1 hour at room temperature, then place in the refrigerator until fully cooled. Cut into squares before serving.

Store leftovers, covered, in the refrigerator for up to 5 days.

SWEET POTATO BLONDIES WITH PECAN STREUSEL

These sweet potato blondies have a rich, almost caramel flavor, thanks to the combination of sweet potato puree and coconut sugar. The almond butter makes them fudgy and the streusel makes them feel like a cross between a coffee cake and a blondie. They're the perfect addition to your holiday table, and also great for a simple afternoon snack.

Yield: 12 to 16 blondies

BLONDIES

1 large egg

⅓ cup (83 g) smooth almond butter

⅓ cup (75 g) sweet potato puree

6 tbsp (84 g) coconut sugar

2 tsp (10 ml) pure vanilla extract

1½ cups (144 g) blanched almond flour

½ tsp baking soda

½ tsp fine sea salt

1 tbsp (6 g) ground cinnamon

STREUSEL

¼ cup (49 g) ghee, at room temperature

1 cup (113 g) chopped pecans

3 tbsp (18 g) blanched almond flour

¼ cup (57 g) coconut sugar

¼ tsp fine sea salt

OPTIONAL MAPLE GLAZE

½ cup (78 g) powdered maple sugar (see page 12)

2–3 tsp (10–15 ml) unsweetened almond milk

½ tsp pure vanilla extract

Prepare the blondies: Preheat your oven to 350°F (177°C) and line an 8-inch (20-cm) square pan with parchment paper on the bottom and up the sides.

In a large bowl, using an electric hand mixer, beat together the egg, almond butter, sweet potato puree, coconut sugar and vanilla.

In a separate bowl, combine the almond flour, baking soda, salt and cinnamon, then stir the dry mixture into the wet, mixing until fully combined.

Transfer the batter to the prepared pan and spread out evenly.

Prepare the streusel: In a medium-sized bowl, combine all the streusel ingredients with a pastry blender or fork until crumbly, then sprinkle all over the batter. Bake for 20 to 22 minutes, or until set in the center and golden brown.

Remove from the oven and allow the pan to cool completely to room temperature before cutting into squares. You can place the pan in the refrigerator to speed up the cooling time.

For the optional glaze: Whisk together the powdered maple sugar, almond milk and vanilla extract until smooth and drizzle all over the bars before or after cutting.

These blondies are best stored, covered, in the refrigerator for up to 5 days.

CHOCOLATE CHIP COOKIE DOUGH STUFFED BROWNIES

The combination of fudgy brownies and chocolate chip cookie dough would definitely be in the dessert hall of fame, if there were one. They're so decadent and rich, no one would even guess they're made with good-for-you ingredients.

Yield: 16 brownies

COOKIE DOUGH

1 cup (96 g) blanched almond flour

3 tbsp (42 g) coconut sugar or maple sugar

2 tbsp (30 ml) melted coconut oil

2 tbsp (30 ml) unsweetened almond milk

1 tsp pure vanilla extract

Pinch of sea salt

⅓ cup (57 g) Paleo-friendly dark chocolate chips, plus more for sprinkling (optional)

BROWNIE BATTER

½ cup (108 g) refined coconut oil

4 oz (113 g) unsweetened baking chocolate, cut into pieces

1 cup (226 g) coconut sugar

2 large eggs, at room temperature

1 large egg yolk, at room temperature

1 tsp pure vanilla extract

¼ cup (25 g) raw cacao powder

½ cup (48 g) blanched almond flour

¼ tsp baking soda

¼ tsp fine sea salt

Prepare the cookie dough: In a medium-sized bowl, stir together all the cookie dough ingredients until a smooth dough forms. Set aside.

Prepare the brownie batter: Preheat your oven to 350°F (177°C) and line an 8-inch (20-cm) square pan with parchment paper on the bottom and up the sides.

In a microwave-safe bowl, combine the coconut oil and unsweetened chocolate. Melt in the microwave in 30-second increments, whisking after each increment, until completely smooth. Whisk in the coconut sugar until completely combined, then the eggs, egg yolk and vanilla. Add the cacao powder, almond flour, baking soda and salt to the chocolate mixture. Mix everything to fully combine.

Spread half of the brownie batter in the prepared pan, then drop the cookie dough evenly all over the batter. Pour the remaining brownie batter over the top, spreading evenly. Sprinkle with extra chocolate chips, if you'd like. Bake for 18 to 20 minutes, or until the center is puffed up and set.

Remove from the oven and allow the pan to cool completely, placing it in the refrigerator for about 1 hour before cutting into squares.

Store leftovers, covered, in the refrigerator for up to 5 days.

VANILLA FROSTED
SUGAR COOKIE BARS

Vanilla lovers everywhere, get exited—because these bars are a dream come true!
They are super kid-friendly with a chewy cookie texture and creamy vanilla frosting,
a cross between a cupcake, blondie and sugar cookie!

Yield: 12 to 16 bars

COOKIE BARS

½ cup (98 g) ghee, at room temperature

⅔ cup (104 g) pure maple sugar

1 tsp pure vanilla extract

1 tsp pure almond extract (optional)

1 large egg, at room temperature

1 large egg yolk, at room temperature

1½ cups (144 g) blanched almond flour

¼ cup (28 g) tapioca flour

½ tsp baking soda

¼ tsp fine sea salt

FROSTING

½ cup (89 g) palm oil shortening, at room temperature

¼ cup (85 g) raw honey

2 tbsp (14 g) tapioca flour

½ tsp pure vanilla extract

Pinch of sea salt

Preheat your oven to 350°F (177°C) and line an 8-inch (20-cm) square pan with parchment paper on the bottom and up the sides.

Prepare the cookie bars: In a large bowl, using an electric mixer, cream together the ghee and maple sugar until creamy, then beat in the vanilla and almond extract (if using). Beat in the egg and egg yolk and mix on medium speed until very smooth.

In a separate medium-sized bowl, combine the almond and tapioca flours, baking soda and salt, then slowly mix the dry mixture into the wet until a sticky batter forms.

Transfer the batter to the prepared pan and bake for 22 to 24 minutes, or until turning light brown and just set in the center.

Remove from the oven and allow the pan to cool completely before frosting. You can place the pan in the refrigerator to speed things up.

Prepare the frosting: In a medium-sized bowl, using an electric hand mixer, beat together the palm oil shortening, honey and tapioca flour until thick and creamy, then beat in the vanilla and salt. Spread the frosting over the completely cooled cookie base, then cut into 12 to 16 squares.

Store leftovers, covered, in the refrigerator for up to 5 days.

CLASSIC HOMEMADE PIES *and* PASTRIES

While testing the recipes for this book, I saved this chapter for last because, frankly, the thought of trying to make authentic Paleo versions of such traditional pies as pecan (page 130), banana cream (page 133), apple (page 120) and Key lime (page 129) felt incredibly intimidating. These are the desserts that you serve to guests at holidays, birthdays and any special social gathering where pie is in demand, so expectations are pretty high for a stellar dessert!

I tested many variations of crust recipes using a combination of almond and tapioca flour with either palm oil shortening, ghee or grass-fed butter for the fat. I came up with a recipe that's as close to a traditional pastry as you'll find. As long as your fat is cold, you can use any of the three, or a combination, for great results. The key here, as with all pastry, is to keep things cold, including chilling the dough well before working with it.

Grain-free dough is always more challenging to work with since it breaks more easily, but the good news is that it's also quite easy to repair and impossible to overwork. Rolling the dough between two sheets of parchment paper is essential, and don't be afraid to use tapioca flour liberally if things get sticky! Once you get used to working with the grain-free dough, the pie-sky is the limit as you make all your family's favorites with clean ingredients.

OUR FAVORITE APPLE PIE

Your classic apple pie is made Paleo-friendly, and it's every bit as delicious, comforting and cozy as the traditional pies you grew up with. I recommend making a faux lattice crust for the top, which looks great yet is actually doable with the easily-broken grain-free dough. This one is too good to wait for Thanksgiving—enjoy it whenever a craving strikes!

Yield: One 9" (23-cm) double-crust pie

DOUBLE PIECRUST

2½ cups (240 g) blanched almond flour

2 cups (224 g) tapioca flour, plus more for sprinkling

1¼ cups (281 g) grass-fed butter, ghee, palm oil shortening or a combination, cold, broken or cut into pieces

1 tsp fine sea salt

2 tbsp (20 g) pure maple or coconut sugar

2 large eggs

Prepare the crust: In the bowl of a food processor, pulse together all the crust ingredients, except the eggs, to create thick crumbs, then add the eggs and pulse until a dough forms. Gather the dough into a ball and split it into 2 mostly equal pieces. Whichever is larger will be the bottom crust; I weigh each portion if I'm unsure. Wrap the dough balls in plastic wrap and flatten them into disks, then chill them while you prepare the apple filling. You can also chill the dough this way until you're ready to use it—simply remove it from the fridge and allow it to sit at room temperature for 20 minutes before using.

Preheat your oven to 400°F (204°C) and have a 9-inch (23-cm) glass pie dish ready before rolling out the dough.

Lay out a sheet of parchment paper and sprinkle generously with tapioca flour. Place the chilled dough on the parchment and sprinkle with more tapioca flour. Cover with another piece of parchment paper and gently roll into an 11- to 12-inch (28- to 30-cm) disk. This dough breaks easily, but it can also be easily repaired and cannot be overworked.

Once rolled out, remove the top piece of parchment paper. Place a 9-inch (23-cm) pie dish upside down over the dough and slide your hand underneath the parchment to flip the dough into the pie dish. Once flipped, slowly remove the parchment paper and gently press the dough into the dish.

(continued)

OUR FAVORITE APPLE PIE (CONT.)

FILLING

6 to 8 apples (I used a mix of Honeycrisp and Granny Smith), peeled, cored and sliced into ¼" to ½" (6- to 13-mm) pieces (about 8 cups [1.4 kg])

2 tbsp (30 ml) fresh lemon juice

1 tbsp (7 g) tapioca or arrowroot flour

6 tbsp (59 g) pure maple sugar

⅛ tsp fine sea salt

½ tsp ground nutmeg

1 tbsp (6 g) ground cinnamon

½ tsp ground ginger

1 tsp pure vanilla extract

1 tbsp (12 g) ghee or grass-fed butter, cold, cut or broken into pieces

EGG WASH

1 large egg

1 tbsp (15 ml) unsweetened almond milk

FOR SERVING

Coconut vanilla ice cream (optional)

Roll out the top crust into another 11- to 12-inch (28- to 30-cm) circle between 2 sheets of parchment paper, dusting with tapioca flour if needed, then carefully place it in the refrigerator and chill until you're ready to top the apple filling.

Prepare the apple filling: In a large bowl, toss the sliced apples with the lemon juice to coat, then toss with all the remaining filling ingredients, except the ghee, to evenly combine. Fill the bottom crust with the apple mixture, layering as desired. Dot the apples on top with the cold ghee.

For a faux lattice top, use a pizza cutter to cut the top crust into strips and crisscross them over the top of the filling without weaving them. Alternatively, you can simply cover the top of the pie with the entire rolled top crust and cut a few slits in it to allow steam to escape. If at any point the dough becomes sticky, place the pie in the freezer for a few minutes before continuing to work. Seal the edges of the dough with your fingers or a fork.

Prepare the egg wash: In a small bowl, whisk together the egg and almond milk and brush it all over the top crust. Place the pie dish on a baking sheet and bake at 400°F (204°C) for 25 minutes. Then, cover the top with aluminum foil and lower the oven temperature to 375°F (191°C). Continue to bake for another 30 to 35 minutes, removing the aluminum foil a few minutes before completely baked to allow the crust to fully brown.

Remove from the oven and allow the pie to cool for at least 45 minutes before serving. Serve with ice cream, if you'd like.

You can let the pie sit at room temperature, loosely covered, overnight if necessary. The apple pie is best served within 24 hours of baking. If you're keeping it longer, cover and refrigerate it until ready to serve, then gently warm in the oven.

BLUEBERRY CRUMB PIE

The crumb topping on this juicy sweet pie not only gives it a nutty crunch, but is also supereasy to make, since there's only a bottom crust to work with. The filling can be sweetened with maple or coconut sugar, and it's thickened perfectly with tapioca flour. Make it à la mode with some coconut vanilla ice cream and watch everyone swoon!

Yield: One 9" (23-cm) pie

CRUST

1¼ cups (120 g) blanched almond flour

¾ cup + 2 tbsp (98 g) tapioca flour, plus more for sprinkling

⅔ cup (150 g) grass-fed butter, ghee or palm oil shortening, cold, broken or cut into pieces

½ tsp fine sea salt

1 tbsp (10 g) pure maple sugar

1 large egg

FILLING

5 cups (850 g) blueberries (if frozen, thaw well before using)

⅓ cup (52 g) pure maple or coconut sugar

2½ tbsp (19 g) tapioca or arrowroot flour

1 tbsp (15 ml) fresh lemon juice

Prepare the crust: In the bowl of a food processor, pulse together all the crust ingredients, except the egg, to create thick crumbs, then add the egg and pulse until a dough forms. Gather the dough into a ball, wrap it in plastic wrap and chill it in the refrigerator for at least 20 minutes prior to rolling or pressing into your pie dish.

Lay out a sheet of parchment paper and sprinkle it generously with tapioca flour. Place the chilled dough on the parchment and sprinkle it with more tapioca flour. Cover with another piece of parchment paper and gently roll into an 11- to 12-inch (28- to 30-cm) disk. This dough breaks easily but it can also be easily repaired. You cannot overwork the dough, so you can always start over if needed.

Once rolled out, remove the top piece of parchment paper. Place a 9-inch (23-cm) pie dish upside down over the dough and slide your hand underneath the parchment to flip the dough into the pie dish. Once flipped, slowly remove the parchment paper and gently press the dough into the dish.

If it's sticky, chill the dough until it's easier to work with. You can crimp the ends, or press with a fork, if desired. Place the dish in the refrigerator to chill while you make the filling and crumble.

Preheat your oven to 400°F (204°C).

Prepare the filling: In a bowl, toss the blueberries with the maple sugar, tapioca flour and lemon juice, then place in the refrigerator to chill while you make the crumble.

(continued)

BLUEBERRY CRUMB PIE (CONT.)

CRUMBLE

6 tbsp (59 g) pure maple sugar

½ cup (48 g) blanched almond flour

1 tsp ground cinnamon

⅓ cup (75 g) grass-fed butter or ghee, cold, broken or cut into pieces

⅔ cup (75 g) chopped walnuts or pecans

FOR SERVING

Coconut whipped cream or ice cream (optional)

Prepare the crumble: In a medium-sized bowl, use a pastry blender or a fork to blend together all the crumble ingredients, except the nuts, until a crumbly mixture forms. Stir in the chopped nuts.

Fill the chilled, unbaked crust with the filling and top with the crumble mixture. Place the pie dish on a large baking sheet and bake for 55 to 60 minutes. After 25 minutes, place a sheet of aluminum foil over the top to avoid excessive browning of the crust and topping.

Remove from the oven and allow the pie to cool completely at room temperature for at least 3 hours so the filling can continue to thicken. Serve with coconut whipped cream or ice cream, if desired.

The pie can be stored, loosely covered, at room temperature for the first day, then covered in the refrigerator for up to 5 days.

TRADITIONAL PUMPKIN PIE

I love that one of my favorite desserts of all time is actually quite simple to make Paleo with just a few adjustments. A grain-free pastry crust is topped with a pumpkin filling sweetened with either maple or coconut sugar and thickened with tapioca flour. Coconut milk makes it extra creamy, and the perfect blend of spices gives it a nostalgic taste that's oh so comforting.

Yield: One 9" (23-cm) pie

CRUST
1¼ cups (120 g) blanched almond flour

¾ cup + 2 tbsp (98 g) tapioca flour, plus more for sprinkling

⅔ cup (150 g) grass-fed butter, ghee or palm oil shortening, cold, broken or cut into pieces

½ tsp fine sea salt

1 tbsp (10 g) pure maple sugar

1 large egg

FILLING
1 (15-oz [425-g]) can pure pumpkin puree

¾ cup (178 ml) canned full-fat coconut milk, blended prior to adding

1 tbsp (7 g) tapioca flour

¾ cup (117 g) pure maple or coconut sugar

2 tsp (10 ml) pure vanilla extract

1 tbsp (7 g) pumpkin pie spice

1 tsp ground cinnamon

½ tsp fine sea salt

3 large eggs, at room temperature

FOR SERVING
Coconut whipped cream (optional)

Preheat your oven to 375°F (191°C).

Prepare the crust: In the bowl of a food processor, pulse together all the crust ingredients except the egg, then add the egg and pulse until a dough forms. Gather the dough into a ball, wrap it in plastic wrap and chill in the refrigerator for at least 20 minutes.

Lay out a sheet of parchment paper and sprinkle generously with tapioca flour. Place the chilled dough on the parchment and sprinkle with more tapioca flour. Cover with another piece of parchment paper and gently roll into an 11- to 12-inch (28- to 30-cm) disk. This dough breaks easily, but it can also be easily repaired and cannot be overworked.

Once rolled out, remove the top piece of parchment paper. Place a 9-inch (23-cm) pie dish upside down over the dough and slide your hand underneath the parchment to flip the dough into the pie dish. Once flipped, slowly remove the parchment paper and gently press the dough into the dish.

If it's sticky, chill the dough until it's easier to work with. You can crimp the ends, or press with a fork, if desired. Use a fork to prick the crust several times so it doesn't puff while baking. Place the crust in the freezer for 10 minutes before baking, to avoid shrinking. Then, bake the crust for 10 minutes, remove from the oven and allow it to partially cool while you make the filling.

Prepare the filling: In a medium-sized bowl, whisk together all the filling ingredients, except the eggs, then whisk in the eggs 1 at a time, being careful not to overmix.

Pour the filling into the partially baked crust, spreading it all around to seal the edges. Place the pie dish on a baking sheet and bake until slightly jiggly in the center, 45 to 50 minutes.

Remove from the oven and allow the pie to cool completely to room temperature, then refrigerate until ready to serve. Serve with a dollop of coconut whipped cream, if desired. Store leftovers, covered, in the refrigerator for up to 5 days.

CREAMY KEY LIME PIE

I struggled with trying to make this Key lime pie true to the traditional recipe, which uses sweetened condensed milk. It felt like a bit too much work to have to make condensed coconut milk from scratch just to use in the pie. What I realized is that you can create a close flavor and texture match by using a combination of honey and coconut cream. Between the sweet-tart creamy filling and the faux graham cracker crust, this pie turned out even better than I hoped!

Yield: One 9" (23-cm) pie

CRUST
1 cup (113 g) walnuts or pecans

1 cup (96 g) blanched almond flour

¼ cup (39 g) pure maple or coconut sugar

1 tsp ground cinnamon

¼ tsp fine sea salt

6 tbsp (90 ml) melted ghee

FILLING
⅔ cup (203 g) coconut cream

½ cup (170 g) raw honey

4 large egg yolks

1 tbsp (6 g) finely grated lime zest

2 tbsp (14 g) tapioca flour

½ cup (119 ml) bottled Key lime juice or fresh lime juice (from 4 to 6 limes)

FOR SERVING
Coconut whipped cream (optional)

Preheat your oven to 350°F (177°C).

Prepare the crust: Use a food processor to pulse the nuts to a fine crumble with a few larger pieces. Stir in the remaining crust ingredients and pulse to form the "graham cracker" dough.

Press the dough into a 9-inch (23-cm) glass pie dish on the bottom and up the sides, pressing down a bit on the edges to make them a uniform thickness and neat. Bake the crust for 10 minutes, or until barely set, then remove from the oven and allow it to cool while you prepare the filling.

Prepare the filling: In a medium-sized bowl, using an electric hand mixer, beat the coconut cream and honey on high speed until creamy, then beat in the egg yolks and lime zest on high speed until thick, about 3 minutes. In a small bowl, stir the tapioca flour into the lime juice. With the mixer on low speed, slowly pour the lime juice mixture into the coconut cream mixture, mixing until just combined—don't overmix.

Pour the filling into the partially cooled crust and bake for 20 to 25 minutes—the filling will still jiggle in the center; it will continue to set as it cools.

Remove from the oven and allow the pie to cool to room temperature on a wire rack, then refrigerate for several hours before serving. Add a dollop of whipped cream when serving, if desired.

Store leftovers, tightly covered, in the refrigerator for up to 4 days.

MAPLE PECAN PIE

This Paleo version of a classic pecan pie uses pure maple syrup instead of corn syrup, giving it a rich flavor with that classic gooey texture. Baked into a perfect grain-free crust, this pecan pie will be a favorite at every gathering.

Yield: One 9" (23-cm) pie

CRUST
1¼ cups (120 g) blanched almond flour

¾ cup + 2 tbsp (98 g) tapioca flour, plus more for sprinkling

⅔ cup (150 g) grass-fed butter, ghee or palm oil shortening, cold, cut or broken into pieces

½ tsp fine sea salt

1 tbsp (10 g) pure maple sugar

1 large egg

FILLING
2½ cups (283 g) pecans

¼ cup (59 ml) melted ghee, slightly cooled

6 tbsp (59 g) pure maple sugar

1½ tbsp (11 g) tapioca or arrowroot flour

2 tsp (10 ml) pure vanilla extract

½ tsp fine sea salt

3 large eggs, at room temperature

1 cup (237 ml) pure maple syrup

Coarse sea salt, for sprinkling

FOR SERVING
Coconut vanilla ice cream (optional)

Prepare the crust: In a food processor, pulse together all the crust ingredients, except the egg. Add the egg and pulse to form a sticky dough. Tightly wrap the dough in plastic wrap and refrigerate for 1 hour or up to overnight.

Preheat your oven to 375°F (191°C).

Lay out a sheet of parchment paper and sprinkle generously with tapioca flour. Place the chilled dough on the parchment and sprinkle with more tapioca flour. Cover with another piece of parchment paper and gently roll into an 11- to 12-inch (28- to 30-cm) disk. This dough breaks easily, but it can also be easily repaired. You cannot overwork the dough, so you can always start over if needed.

Once rolled out, remove the top piece of parchment paper. Place your pie dish upside down over the dough and slide your hand underneath the parchment to flip the dough into the pie dish. Once flipped, slowly remove the parchment paper and gently press the dough into the dish.

If it's sticky, chill the dough until it's easier to work with. You can crimp the ends, or press with a fork, if desired. Use a fork to prick the crust several times so it doesn't puff while baking. Place the crust in the freezer for at least 10 minutes before baking, to prevent shrinking. After, bake the crust for 10 minutes, then remove from the oven and allow it to partially cool while you make the filling. Lower the oven temperature to 350°F (177°C).

Prepare the filling: Spread the pecans inside the warm piecrust and set the pie dish aside. In a large bowl, whisk together the ghee, maple sugar and tapioca flour until smooth. Then, whisk in the vanilla, salt, eggs and maple syrup until combined. Pour the mixture evenly over the pecans.

Bake the pie for 40 to 50 minutes, or until lightly browned and set.

Remove from the oven and allow the pie to cool at room temperature. You can also refrigerate the pie to speed up the cooling time. Serve at room temperature. Sprinkle with coarse sea salt and serve with ice cream, if desired.

Store leftovers, tightly covered, in the refrigerator for up to 5 days.

BANANA CREAM PIE

This recipe uses my go-to piecrust as a base for layers of sweet bananas, vanilla custard and coconut whipped cream that come together to create an insanely irresistible dessert. After assembling the layers, it's best to chill the pie overnight for easy slicing. This pie was a hit with my entire family—even the banana haters!

Yield: One 9" (23-cm) pie

WHIPPED TOPPING
1 cup (237 ml) coconut cream

3 tbsp (14 g) tapioca flour

1½ tbsp (32 g) raw honey

½ tsp pure vanilla extract

CRUST
1¼ cups (120 g) blanched almond flour

¾ cup + 2 tbsp (98 g) tapioca flour, plus more for dusting

½ cup (113 g) grass-fed butter, ghee or palm oil shortening, cold, broken or cut into pieces

½ tsp fine sea salt

1 tbsp (10 g) pure maple sugar

1 large egg

Prepare the whipped topping: In a large bowl, combine the coconut cream and tapioca flour and, using an electric hand mixer, beat on medium speed until creamy. Add the honey and vanilla and continue to beat until smooth. Cover with plastic wrap and refrigerate until ready to serve.

Prepare the crust: In a food processor, pulse together all the crust ingredients, except the egg, to form a crumbly mixture. Add the egg and pulse to form a sticky dough. Tightly wrap the dough in plastic wrap and refrigerate for 1 hour or up to overnight.

Preheat your oven to 375°F (191°C).

Lay out a sheet of parchment paper and sprinkle generously with tapioca flour. Place the chilled dough on the parchment and sprinkle with more tapioca flour. Cover with another piece of parchment paper and gently roll into an 11- to 12-inch (28- to 30-cm) disk. This dough breaks easily, but it can also be easily repaired. You cannot overwork the dough, so you can always start over if needed.

Once rolled out, remove the top piece of parchment paper. Place a 9-inch (23-cm) pie dish upside down over the dough and slide your hand underneath the parchment to flip the dough into the pie dish. Once flipped, slowly remove the parchment paper and gently press the dough into the dish.

If it's sticky, chill until it's easier to work with. You can crimp the ends, or press with a fork, if desired. Use a fork to prick the crust several times so it doesn't puff while baking. Place the dish in the freezer to chill for 10 minutes. Once chilled, bake for 20 minutes, or until light golden brown. Remove from the oven and allow to cool to room temperature on a wire rack.

(continued)

BANANA CREAM PIE (CONT.)

FILLING

1½ cups (356 ml) coconut milk, blended prior to adding

1 cup (237 ml) coconut cream

6 tbsp (128 g) raw honey

⅓ cup (37 g) tapioca flour

½ tsp fine sea salt

4 large egg yolks, whisked

3 tbsp (37 g) ghee

1½ tsp (8 ml) pure vanilla extract

FOR ASSEMBLING

2 large, firm bananas

Prepare the filling: In a large saucepan, combine the coconut milk, coconut cream, honey, tapioca flour and salt and whisk to dissolve the tapioca flour.

Place the pan over medium-high heat and cook, whisking constantly, for 5 minutes to bring to a boil. Lower the heat to medium and continue to whisk at a boil for 5 minutes, then remove from the heat.

Slowly stream a small amount of the hot mixture into the bowl with the whisked egg yolks while whisking constantly. This is called tempering the eggs. Add the tempered egg yolk mixture to the saucepan, whisking constantly, until incorporated. Place back over medium heat and continue to cook, stirring, to bring back to a boil, then continue to cook for 2 to 3 minutes. Remove the mixture from the heat and stir in the ghee and vanilla.

Pour the custard into a bowl and lay a piece of plastic wrap onto the top of the custard to prevent a film from forming. Refrigerate for 1 hour.

After the custard has cooled, assemble the pie: Slice one of the bananas and arrange the slices on the bottom of the cooled crust, then pour the custard over them, smoothing the top. Place another piece of plastic wrap over the custard and refrigerate overnight for best results.

Before serving, spread the whipped topping over the top. Slice the second banana and arrange the slices over the whipped topping.

Store leftovers in the refrigerator for up to 3 days.

SILKY DARK CHOCOLATE CREAM PIE

I obviously couldn't allow the pie chapter of this book to leave out chocolate—so here we are with this incredibly rich, dark chocolate cream pie. The method for the filling is very similar to that of the Banana Cream Pie (page 133), and the result is a thick, creamy chocolate custard over a classic pastry crust that also happens to be grain-free, dairy-free and refined sugar–free.

Yield: One 9" (23-cm) pie

WHIPPED TOPPING

1 cup (237 ml) coconut cream

3 tbsp (21 g) tapioca flour

1½ tbsp (32 g) raw honey

½ tsp pure vanilla extract

CRUST

1¼ cups (120 g) blanched almond flour

¾ cup + 2 tbsp (98 g) tapioca flour, plus more for sprinkling

½ tsp fine sea salt

1 tbsp (15 ml) pure maple syrup

½ cup (113 g) grass-fed butter, ghee or palm oil shortening, cold, broken or cut into pieces

1 large egg

Prepare the whipped topping: In a large bowl, using an electric hand mixer, combine the coconut cream and tapioca flour and beat on medium speed until creamy. Add the honey and vanilla and continue to beat until smooth. Cover with plastic wrap and refrigerate until ready to serve.

Prepare the crust: In a food processor, pulse together all the crust ingredients, except the egg, to form a crumbly mixture. Add the egg and pulse to form a sticky dough. Tightly wrap the dough in plastic wrap and refrigerate for 1 hour or up to overnight.

Preheat your oven to 375°F (191°C).

Lay out a sheet of parchment paper and sprinkle generously with tapioca flour. Place the chilled dough on the parchment and sprinkle with more tapioca flour. Cover with another piece of parchment paper and gently roll into an 11- to 12-inch (28- to 30-cm) disk. This dough breaks easily, but it can also be easily repaired. You cannot overwork the dough, so you can always start over if needed.

Once rolled out, remove the top piece of parchment paper. Place a 9-inch (23-cm) pie dish upside down over the dough and slide your hand underneath the parchment to flip the dough into the pie dish. Once flipped, slowly remove the parchment paper and gently press the dough into the dish.

If it's sticky, chill the dough until it's easier to work with. You can crimp the ends, or press with a fork, if desired. Use a fork to prick the crust several times so it doesn't puff while baking. Place the dish in the freezer for 10 minutes. Once chilled, bake for 20 minutes, or until light golden brown. Remove from the oven and allow to cool to room temperature on a wire rack.

(continued)

SILKY DARK CHOCOLATE CREAM PIE (CONT.)

FILLING

8 oz (227 g) unsweetened baking chocolate, chopped

2 tbsp (24 g) ghee

1 tsp pure vanilla extract

¾ cup (117 g) pure maple or coconut sugar

3 tbsp (21 g) tapioca flour

⅛ tsp fine sea salt

3 cups (711 ml) canned full-fat coconut milk, blended prior to adding, divided

3 large egg yolks

¼ cup (59 ml) pure maple syrup

Prepare the filling: In a large bowl, combine the baking chocolate, ghee and vanilla and set aside.

In a medium-sized saucepan, whisk together the maple sugar, tapioca flour and salt. Whisk in ¼ cup (59 ml) of the coconut milk until the mixture is smooth, with no lumps. Repeat with another ¼ cup (59 ml) of the coconut milk, then whisk in the egg yolks.

Place the saucepan over medium heat and gradually whisk in the remaining 2½ cups (593 ml) of coconut milk and the maple syrup. Bring to a boil, whisking constantly as the mixture thickens; boil for 1 minute.

Remove the pan from the heat and pour the coconut milk mixture over the chocolate mixture, whisking until the chocolate is melted and the filling is smooth. If your mixture has lumps, you can pass the filling through a strainer into a bowl—this is optional. Scrape the underside of the strainer once in a while with a clean spatula to help the process along.

Place plastic wrap on the surface of the filling to prevent a skin from forming, then chill for 1 hour.

To assemble the pie, spoon the cooled filling into the cooled, baked piecrust. Smooth the top with a spatula or spoon. Place another piece of plastic wrap over the filling and chill for 4 hours or overnight.

Once ready to serve, spread the whipped topping over the top or simply dollop it on each piece as you serve.

Store leftovers, covered, in the refrigerator for up to 3 days.

SCONES, SWEET BREADS *and* OTHER BREAKFAST GOODIES

By now you should be asking yourself, "but where are the scones, donuts and cinnamon rolls?!" and the answer is right here in this chapter! The two donut recipes in this chapter are the biggest hit with my family, and in truth I can't blame them—the Chocolate-Frosted Donuts (page 140) are so close to the "real" version that it's scary—in a good way, of course!

We also have easy, no-yeast cinnamon rolls (page 144)—baked in a muffin pan to avoid the issue of spreading too much, which often happens with grain-free cinnamon rolls. And yes—I also had to include hand pies! Given how many store-bought Pop-Tarts I consumed as a child, I knew I couldn't skip them in this book. My Homemade Apple Cinnamon Hand Pies (page 148) are similar to apple pie, but of course portable and maybe just a little bit more fun.

Lastly, the Blueberry Scones (page 143) are definitely one of my prouder Paleo baking moments and one of my favorite recipes in the book. No matter what your breakfast craving, I know you'll find something in this chapter to make any morning a whole lot sweeter.

CHOCOLATE-FROSTED DONUTS

Although my dad didn't bake, he definitely instilled a love for dessert in me. I have fond memories of going out to the store on Saturday nights and loading up on chocolate-frosted donuts and chocolate cake. The cake was for him, the donuts for me. Now that I think of it, I bet he snuck a donut in there, too. Either way, I knew I had to create a healthier version of one of my favorite childhood treats! This one is a hands-down favorite for my kids, too.

Yield: 8 donuts

DONUTS
Coconut oil spray

1½ cups (144 g) blanched almond flour

¼ cup (28 g) tapioca flour

½ tsp baking soda

½ tsp aluminum-free baking powder or homemade Paleo baking powder (see page 12)

¼ tsp fine sea salt

2 large eggs

¼ cup (59 ml) canned full-fat coconut milk, blended prior to adding

⅔ cup (158 ml) pure maple syrup

3 tbsp (45 ml) melted coconut oil, cooled

1 tsp pure vanilla extract

GLAZE
⅓ cup (59 g) palm oil shortening or ghee

3 tbsp (16 g) raw cacao powder

3 tbsp (45 ml) pure maple syrup

¼ tsp pure vanilla extract

FOR TOPPING
Chopped nuts (optional)

Prepare the donuts: Preheat your oven to 350°F (177°C) and lightly spray 8 wells of a silicone or nonstick donut pan with coconut oil spray.

In a medium-sized bowl, combine the almond and tapioca flours, baking soda, baking powder and salt.

In a separate medium bowl, whisk together the eggs, coconut milk, maple syrup, coconut oil and vanilla, then whisk the dry mixture into the wet until fully combined and a thick batter forms.

Transfer all the dough to a large plastic bag, cut a ½- to 1-inch (1.3- to 2.5-cm) hole in the corner and pipe the batter into the prepared donut molds. Bake for 15 minutes, or until a toothpick inserted into a donut comes out clean.

Remove from the oven and allow to cool for at least 5 minutes in the pan, then release each donut carefully onto a wire rack and let cool completely.

While the donuts cool, make the glaze: In a small saucepan, melt the palm oil shortening over very low heat until almost melted, then whisk in the cacao powder and maple syrup until a shiny glaze forms. Remove from the heat and stir in the vanilla.

Glaze the donuts immediately by drizzling or spreading with a spoon or spatula. Allow the glaze to cool before serving; it will remain soft but solid at room temperature. While the glaze is still wet, you can sprinkle with chopped nuts, if desired.

Store leftovers, loosely covered, at room temperature for up to 2 days, then cover and refrigerate to keep them longer.

BLUEBERRY SCONES

Creating the perfect Paleo scone is no easy task. The dough requires lots of chilling and can be difficult to work with, and it's easy to wind up with something that's too moist or too dry and crumbly. But here, I have cracked the code for delicious grain-free scones with juicy blueberries that are perfect for a fun weekend breakfast or brunch treat.

Yield: 8 scones

1¾ cups (168 g) blanched almond flour

¾ cup (84 g) tapioca flour, plus more for sprinkling

¼ cup (32 g) coconut flour

1½ tsp (6 g) aluminum-free baking powder or homemade Paleo baking powder (see page 12)

½ tsp baking soda

½ tsp fine sea salt

½ cup (78 g) pure maple sugar

⅔ cup (118 g) palm oil shortening or ghee, cold, broken into pieces

½ cup (119 ml) canned full-fat coconut milk, blended prior to adding

1 tsp pure almond or vanilla extract

1 large egg

¾ cup (128 g) blueberries

OPTIONAL MAPLE GLAZE
½ cup (78 g) powdered maple sugar (see page 12)

2–3 tsp (10–15 ml) unsweetened almond milk

½ tsp pure vanilla extract

In a large bowl, stir together the almond, tapioca and coconut flours plus the baking powder, baking soda, salt and maple sugar.

Add the palm oil shortening and blend with a fork or pastry blender until an evenly crumbly mixture forms. This can also be done by pulsing a few times in a food processor.

Make a well in the center of the crumbly mixture and add the coconut milk, almond extract and egg. Stir well until no flour spots show—you should have a sticky dough.

Stir in the blueberries, then place the bowl in the freezer to chill for 30 minutes.

Meanwhile, preheat your oven to 400°F (204°C) and line a large baking sheet with parchment paper.

Sprinkle some tapioca flour on the prepared baking sheet and place the chilled dough on top. Wet your hands lightly and work the dough into a 7- to 8-inch (18- to 20-cm) disk.

Using a very sharp knife, cut the dough into 8 triangular wedges. Wet the knife to help it glide more easily through the dough. If the dough becomes sticky, place it in the freezer to chill again for 5 minutes. Separate the wedges carefully with a rubber spatula or your hands and place them about 2 inches (5 cm) apart on the baking sheet.

Bake for 16 to 18 minutes, or until set and golden brown. The scones are best served warm.

For the optional glaze: Whisk together the powdered maple sugar, almond milk and vanilla until smooth and drizzle all over the scones before or after cutting.

Store the scones, loosely covered, at room temperature for 1 day, or wrap tightly and freeze, once cooled, to keep them for longer.

EASY CINNAMON ROLLS (IN A MUFFIN PAN!)

Classic grain-free cinnamon rolls made even better in a muffin pan—who knew?! Each roll is popped in a well-greased muffin pan for a fun twist. The icing is incredibly rich and delicious, making these cinnamon rolls perfect for a gooey brunch treat or dessert.

Yield: 12 cinnamon rolls

ROLLS
1¾ cups (168 g) almond flour

1½ cups (168 g) tapioca flour, plus more for sprinkling

¾ tsp baking soda

¾ tsp fine sea salt

⅓ cup (79 ml) light coconut milk, blended

3 tbsp (45 ml) melted ghee or grass-fed butter

2 tbsp (30 ml) raw honey, melted

1 tsp pure vanilla extract

1 large egg, at room temperature

Coconut or avocado oil spray

FILLING
1 tbsp (12 g) ghee, at room temperature

1 tbsp (21 g) raw honey, at room temperature

2 tsp (4 g) ground cinnamon

TOPPING
¾ cup (117 g) powdered maple sugar (see page 12)

1 tbsp (11 g) palm oil shortening or ghee, at room temperature

½ tsp pure vanilla extract

1 tbsp (15 ml) coconut or unsweetened almond milk

Prepare the rolls: In a large bowl, combine the almond and tapioca flours, baking soda and salt. Add the coconut milk, ghee, honey and vanilla and mix well. Lastly, add the egg and continue to mix until a sticky dough forms.

Chill the dough in the refrigerator for 10 to 15 minutes. At this point, it should be firm enough to handle with some help from extra tapioca flour.

Meanwhile, preheat your oven to 350°F (177°C) and spray 12 wells of a muffin pan with coconut or avocado oil spray.

Sprinkle about 1 tablespoon (7 g) of tapioca flour over a large piece of parchment paper, placed on a large cutting board (so you can transport the dough to the freezer easily), and place the dough in the center.

Sprinkle more tapioca on your hands and press the dough into a long rectangle—about 14 x 6 inches (35 x 15 cm). At any point that the dough becomes too soft or sticky to work with, you can chill it in the refrigerator for a few minutes before continuing. I find that using the heel of my hand to work the dough into this shape is most efficient.

Prepare the filling: In a small bowl, mix together the ghee and honey, spread it all over the dough, then sprinkle all over with the cinnamon.

Using the parchment paper to help you, roll the dough tightly on the long side, so that your roll is about 14 inches (35 cm) long. Once rolled, place the dough in the freezer for 5 minutes for easier slicing.

Using a sharp knife, slice the roll into 12 pieces and place each, flat side down, in a prepared muffin well. Bake for 16 to 18 minutes, or until the tops are golden brown and a toothpick inserted in the center of a roll comes out clean.

While the rolls bake, prepare the topping: In a small bowl, stir together the powdered maple sugar, palm oil shortening and vanilla, then add the coconut milk slowly until your desired consistency is achieved. For best results, the cinnamon rolls should be iced and served while still warm.

MAPLE CINNAMON DONUTS

If you're a cinnamon lover, these donuts are your new best friend and favorite sweet treat—easy to make, even easier to eat and loaded with cinnamon and maple sugar flavor. I topped them with a maple icing for an extra-special treat, but they're perfectly delicious and sweet with just the cinnamon sugar dusting, if you prefer.

Yield: 8 donuts

DOUGH
Coconut oil spray

1½ cups (144 g) blanched almond flour

¼ cup (28 g) tapioca flour

½ tsp baking soda

½ tsp aluminum-free baking powder or homemade Paleo baking powder (see page 12)

¼ tsp fine sea salt

2 tsp (4 g) ground cinnamon

½ tsp ground nutmeg

2 large eggs

¼ cup (59 ml) canned full-fat coconut milk, blended prior to adding

¼ cup (59 ml) pure maple syrup

¼ cup (57 g) coconut sugar

3 tbsp (45 ml) melted coconut oil, cooled

1 tsp pure vanilla extract

CINNAMON SUGAR TOPPING
2 tbsp (20 g) pure maple or coconut sugar

¾ tsp ground cinnamon

OPTIONAL ICING
⅓ cup (52 g) powdered maple sugar (see page 12)

½ tsp ground cinnamon

½ tsp pure vanilla extract

3–4 tsp (15–20 ml) coconut or unsweetened almond milk

Prepare the dough: Preheat your oven to 350°F (177°C) and prepare your donut pan by lightly spraying with coconut oil spray.

In a medium-sized bowl, combine the almond and tapioca flours, baking soda, baking powder, salt, cinnamon and nutmeg.

In a separate medium-sized bowl, whisk together the eggs, coconut milk, maple syrup, coconut sugar, coconut oil and vanilla, then whisk the dry mixture into the wet until fully combined and a thick batter forms.

Transfer the dough to a large plastic bag, cut a ½- to 1-inch (1.3- to 2.5-cm) hole in the corner and pipe the batter into the prepared molds. Bake for 15 minutes, or until a toothpick inserted into a donut comes out clean.

Remove from the oven and allow the donuts to cool for at least 5 minutes in the pan, then release each donut carefully onto a wire rack and let cool completely.

Prepare the cinnamon sugar topping: In a small bowl, combine the maple sugar and cinnamon, then dust or sprinkle all over the tops of the donuts.

For the optional icing: In a separate small bowl, whisk all the icing ingredients together, adding the coconut milk slowly until you get the right consistency for drizzling. Drizzle over the donuts before serving. The icing will harden after about 30 minutes at room temperature.

Store leftovers, loosely covered, at room temperature for up to 2 days, then cover and refrigerate to keep longer.

HOMEMADE APPLE CINNAMON HAND PIES

I won't claim that this is one of the easier recipes in the book; however, it's definitely not difficult if you're patient in working with the dough. This pastry dough is higher in fat content than my others, which produced a superior texture after baking that I couldn't resist. The gooey sweet apple filling and cinnamon icing make these homemade hand pies well worth the effort!

Yield: 9 hand pies

FILLING

2 cups (240 g) peeled, cored and chopped Pink Lady or other crisp, tart, sweet apple

¼ cup (57 g) coconut sugar

2 tsp (10 ml) fresh lemon juice

2 tsp (4 g) ground cinnamon

⅛ tsp fine sea salt

DOUGH

2 cups (192 g) blanched almond flour

2 cups (224 g) tapioca flour, plus more for sprinkling

1 tsp fine sea salt

2 tbsp (20 g) pure maple or coconut sugar

1½ cups (338 g) grass-fed butter or ghee, cold, cut or broken into pieces

2 large eggs

Prepare the filling: In a medium-sized saucepan, combine all the filling ingredients over medium heat. Cook, stirring, until the sugar has dissolved and the apple juices begin to release, about 5 minutes. Continue to cook until the apples soften, 3 to 4 minutes more. Remove the pan from the heat.

Prepare the dough: In the bowl of a food processor, pulse together all the dough ingredients, except the eggs, to create thick crumbs, then add the eggs and process until a dough forms.

Gather the dough with a spatula and divide into 2 equal parts. The dough will be sticky. Wrap each portion in plastic wrap and flatten into disks, then chill in the refrigerator for 30 minutes or up to overnight.

When ready to bake, place a sheet of parchment paper on a large cutting board and sprinkle generously with tapioca flour. Place 1 dough disk on the parchment and sprinkle with more tapioca flour, then top with another piece of parchment. Roll out the dough, starting from the center and moving outward, into a 9 x 12–inch (23 x 30–cm) rectangle that is ⅛ to ¼ inch (3 to 6 mm) thick. Use a pizza cutter to clean up the edges of the rectangle.

If the dough became very soft, chill it in the fridge or freezer for a couple of minutes before proceeding.

After rolling out, leave the dough on the parchment paper and carefully transfer the parchment to a large baking sheet. Use the pizza cutter to cut the dough into 9 rectangles, approximately 3 x 4 inches (7.5 x 10 cm). Gently separate the rectangles from one another—½ inch (1.3 cm) of space around each is enough.

Place the entire baking sheet in the refrigerator to chill while you repeat the steps with the remaining disk of dough and a second large baking sheet.

(continued)

HOMEMADE APPLE CINNAMON HAND PIES (CONT.)

EGG WASH

1 large egg

1 tbsp (15 ml) water, unsweetened almond milk or coconut milk

ICING

½ cup (78 g) powdered maple sugar (see page 12)

½ tsp ground cinnamon

½ tsp pure vanilla extract

3–4 tsp (15–20 ml) coconut or unsweetened almond milk

Assemble the hand pies: Preheat your oven to 350°F (177°C) and place an oven rack in the top half of your oven.

Spoon about 1½ tablespoons (23 g) of the apple filling in the center of one pan's worth of rectangles (9 rectangles), spreading out gently and leaving a ½-inch (1.3-cm) border of unfilled dough. Carefully top each filled rectangle with an unfilled rectangle from the second pan of dough. Dipping a fork in tapioca flour, lightly seal the edges of the hand pies. Prick the top of each pastry with the fork to allow steam to release while baking.

Prepare the egg wash: In a small bowl, whisk together the egg and water and lightly brush it over the tops of the hand pies.

Bake for 20 to 22 minutes, or until just beginning to turn golden brown. Remove from the oven and place the entire baking sheet on a wire rack to cool completely.

While the hand pies cool, prepare the icing: In a small bowl, whisk together all the icing ingredients. Drizzle the icing over the completely cooled hand pies, then allow it to harden for 20 minutes before serving.

Store leftovers, covered, in the refrigerator for up to 1 week, or freeze them to keep longer.

ORANGE CRANBERRY PECAN ROLLS

These rolls are a citrusy spin on the classic cinnamon rolls from my blog. It's important to try to roll the dough up as tightly as possible to make sure your rolls don't spread out a lot while baking. They're best served warm but can also be frozen if you want to save some for later—just thaw them at room temperature and warm them a bit in the toaster oven.

Yield: 9 rolls

DOUGH

1⅔ cups (160 g) blanched almond flour

1½ cups (168 g) tapioca flour, plus more for sprinkling

½ tsp baking soda

¾ tsp fine sea salt

⅓ cup (79 ml) melted ghee or grass-fed butter

⅓ cup (79 ml) fresh orange juice

Zest of 1 large orange, plus more for garnish (optional)

2 tbsp (30 ml) pure maple syrup

1 tsp pure vanilla extract

½ tsp pure almond extract

1 large egg, at room temperature

FILLING

1 tbsp (15 ml) pure maple syrup

1½ tsp (3 g) ground cinnamon

¼ cup (39 g) chopped pecans, plus more for garnish (optional)

¼ cup (38 g) dried cranberries

Prepare the dough: In a large bowl, combine the almond and tapioca flours, baking soda and salt.

In a medium-sized bowl, combine the ghee, orange juice and zest, maple syrup, vanilla and almond extract. Pour the wet mixture into the dry and stir until fully combined. Add the egg and continue to mix until a sticky dough forms.

Chill the dough in the refrigerator for 15 minutes. At this point, it should be firm enough to handle with some help from extra tapioca flour.

Sprinkle about 1 tablespoon (7 g) of tapioca flour over a large piece of parchment paper, placed on either a large cutting board or baking sheet, then place the dough in the center.

Sprinkle more tapioca flour on your hands and gently press the dough into a rectangle—about 10 x 7 inches (25 x 18 cm). I find that using the heel of my hand to work the dough into this shape is most efficient.

Once the dough rectangle has been formed, prepare the filling: Drizzle the maple syrup all over the dough, then use a pastry brush to spread it evenly. Sprinkle with the cinnamon, then arrange the pecans and cranberries over the cinnamon layer.

Roll up the dough along the long edge (so your roll is 10 inches [25 cm] long), using the parchment paper that's underneath to help you carefully roll it as tightly as possible. A tight roll is essential to getting the rolls to bake properly. You won't be rolling the parchment *with* the dough; rather, using it to guide the dough so you don't have to touch it.

Once rolled, gently seal the end and immediately transfer the roll to the freezer to chill for 10 to 15 minutes (it will have softened a lot at this point), so you can easily cut it.

While the dough chills, preheat your oven to 350°F (177°C) and line a large baking sheet with parchment paper.

(continued)

ORANGE CRANBERRY PECAN ROLLS (CONT.)

GLAZE

6 tbsp (90 ml) coconut cream

1 tbsp (15 ml) fresh orange juice

2 tbsp (30 ml) pure maple syrup

½ tsp pure vanilla extract

Pinch of sea salt

After chilling, using a very sharp knife, cut the roll into 1- to 1½-inch (2.5- to 4-cm) sections and place each, flat side down, on the prepared baking sheet. You should have 9 individual rolls. Bake in the middle rack of the oven for 20 minutes, or until beginning to turn golden brown.

Prepare the glaze: In a small saucepan, bring the coconut cream, orange juice and maple syrup to a boil. Lower the heat and allow it to simmer at a low boil, stirring occasionally, for 5 to 10 minutes, or until syrupy (like sweetened condensed milk). Then remove from the heat and stir in the vanilla and salt. It will thicken as it cools. Allow it to cool completely before drizzling over the rolls. You can also refrigerate the glaze to speed up the cooling and thickening.

Prior to serving (remember to serve them warm!), drizzle the glaze all over the rolls, using a spoon. Add more chopped pecans and orange zest as desired.

If you aren't serving the rolls warm, they can be tightly wrapped, without the glaze, and frozen for later use. Simply thaw at room temperature, then gently warm in the oven or toaster oven before drizzling with the glaze.

SAVORY PALEO BAKING

Even though this book is almost entirely dessert recipes, I couldn't leave out a few of my favorite savory baked goods, such as Classic Chewy Homemade Bagels (page 159), (insanely good!) Authentic Soft Pretzels (page 160) and a Hearty Paleo Sandwich Bread (page 156).

This chapter was my favorite to work on because my family went wild over every single recipe. In fact, they legit questioned whether I actually made the bagels myself or bought them from a store—I mean, really—that is how authentic they taste!

This is the only chapter where I used yeast for a couple of the recipes. Good news, though—not only is yeast Paleo-friendly, but in my recipes, you only need to add it to the dry ingredients and proceed as usual—there is no rise time *at all!* Whether you make the soft pretzels as a fun weekend baking project or put the sandwich bread on a weekly rotation, I know you're going to enjoy baking these savory goodies.

HEARTY PALEO SANDWICH BREAD

This bread is easy to make, hearty yet also fluffy and perfect for any type of sandwich! You can toast it and make breakfast sandwiches, have a BLT or top it with almond butter, fruit preserves and bananas for a healthy grain-free and Paleo treat.

Yield: 1 medium-sized loaf (12 servings)

1¾ cups (168 g) blanched almond flour

1 cup (112 g) tapioca flour

¾ cup (124 g) golden flaxseed meal

2 tsp (8 g) aluminum-free baking powder or homemade Paleo baking powder (see page 12)

½ tsp baking soda

¾ tsp fine sea salt

3 large eggs

2 large egg whites

2 tsp (10 ml) pure maple syrup

¼ cup (59 ml) unsweetened almond milk

¼ cup (59 ml) avocado or olive oil

2 tsp (10 ml) raw apple cider vinegar

Preheat your oven to 350°F (177°C) and line an 8½ x 4½–inch (22 x 11–cm) loaf pan with parchment paper.

In a large bowl, combine the almond and tapioca flours, flaxseed meal, baking powder, baking soda and salt, then set aside.

In a separate large bowl, whisk together the eggs, egg whites, maple syrup, almond milk, avocado oil and vinegar. Immediately stir the dry mixture into the wet, stirring until moistened, being careful not to overmix.

Transfer the batter to the prepared loaf pan and spread out evenly, tapping the pan on the countertop a few times to evenly distribute.

Bake for 50 to 60 minutes, or until deep golden brown.

Remove from the oven and allow to cool in the pan on a wire rack for about 30 minutes, then remove from the pan holding the sides of the parchment paper and continue to cool on the rack until fully cooled.

Slice as desired and store leftovers, covered tightly, in the refrigerator for up to 4 days; you can also freeze this bread to keep it longer.

CLASSIC CHEWY HOMEMADE BAGELS

Growing up in New York, I admit I became a complete bagel snob by the age of five, and even after eating Paleo for so long, I still have my original bagel standards. I knew I had to create a real-deal New York–style bagel recipe for this book, and after a few tries, my whole family was blown away by the result. They're dense and chewy with a golden crust and are perfect for breakfast sandwiches, with cold cuts or even just plain!

Yield: 8 bagels

DOUGH
1 cup (96 g) blanched almond flour

3 cups (336 g) tapioca flour, plus more for sprinkling

½ cup (83 g) golden flaxseed meal

1½ tsp (7 g) fine sea salt

1 (2¼-tsp [7-g]) packet instant yeast

2 tbsp (43 g) raw honey

2 large eggs

1 tbsp (15 ml) olive or avocado oil

¾ cup (178 ml) water, at room temperature

Coconut or avocado oil spray

FOR BOILING
2 qt (1.9 L) water

¼ cup (85 g) raw honey

EGG WASH
1 large egg white

1 tbsp (15 ml) water

OPTIONAL TOPPINGS
Everything bagel seasoning, poppy seeds or sesame seeds

Prepare the dough: In the bowl of a stand mixer fitted with the paddle attachment, combine the almond and tapioca flours, flaxseed meal, salt and yeast and mix on low speed until well mixed.

Create a well in the center of the dry mixture and add the honey, eggs, olive oil and water. Mix on medium speed until fully combined. Cover the bowl and place in the refrigerator to chill for 10 to 15 minutes.

While the dough chills, preheat your oven to 400°F (204°C) and, in a large pot, bring the water and honey to a boil. Line a large baking sheet with parchment paper and spray with coconut or avocado oil spray.

Remove the dough from the refrigerator and place it on a cutting board lined with parchment paper. Sprinkle tapioca flour over the parchment. Shape the dough into 8 rounds that are 3 inches (7.5 cm) in diameter by 2 inches (5 cm) high. Use your finger to make a hole in the center of each round, poking all the way through. Make sure the bagels aren't shaped too flat.

Once the water is boiling, carefully drop the bagels in, 2 or 3 at a time, making sure they have enough room to float. Boil for 1 minute on each side, then, using a wide slotted spatula, carefully remove each bagel and place on the prepared baking sheet. Repeat until all the bagels are boiled.

Prepare the egg wash: In a small bowl, whisk together the egg white and water, then use a pastry brush to brush on top and around the sides of each bagel. Sprinkle the bagels with whatever toppings you like—everything bagel seasoning, poppy seeds, sesame seeds—or keep them plain.

Place the baking sheet on the upper middle rack and bake for 20 minutes, rotating the pan once for even browning.

Remove from the oven and transfer the bagels to wire racks to cool. These bagels are best served fresh, but you can also freeze them within a few hours of making them to keep them for a longer period of time.

AUTHENTIC SOFT PRETZELS

I can still hardly believe how true to the original these Paleo soft pretzels taste.
They are perhaps my proudest recipe-testing moment, with their crusty outside and
dense yet soft and chewy middle. They're amazing brushed with a little melted ghee
after baking for that extra-buttery "mall pretzel" flavor.

Yield: 9 pretzels

DOUGH
1 cup (96 g) blanched almond flour

3 cups (336 g) tapioca flour

½ cup (83 g) golden flaxseed meal

1 (2¼-tsp [7-g]) packet instant yeast

1 tbsp (14 g) coconut sugar

1½ tsp (7 g) fine sea salt

2 tbsp (30 ml) melted ghee

¾ cup + 1 tbsp (193 ml) water, at room temperature

2 large eggs, at room temperature

FOR BOILING
½ cup (115 g) baking soda

9 cups (2 L) water

EGG WASH
1 large egg

1 tbsp (15 ml) unsweetened almond milk

Coarse sea salt, for sprinkling

Melted ghee, for brushing (optional)

Prepare the dough: Preheat your oven to 400°F (204°C) and line 2 large baking sheets with parchment paper. Arrange 2 oven racks in the upper half of your oven.

In a stand mixer fitted with the paddle or dough hook attachment, mix together the almond and tapioca flours, flaxseed, yeast, sugar and salt.

Make a well in the center of the dry mixture and add the ghee, water and eggs, mixing on low to medium speed until a thick dough forms. Remove the bowl from the mixer, cover with plastic wrap and refrigerate for 10 minutes.

While the dough is chilling, prepare to boil the pretzels: In a large stockpot, mix together the baking soda and water and bring to a boil.

After the dough chills, divide it into 9 equal segments. If the dough seems dry or crumbly, add a drop of water to make it more pliable. If it's sticky, add a bit more tapioca flour with your hands to make it workable.

Gently shape a segment into a rope about 15 inches (38 cm) long. Bring the ends up and together so the dough forms a circle. Twist the ends, then bring them down toward you and gently press down to create the pretzel shape. Repeat the process for all 9 pretzels.

To boil the pretzels, gently lower 2 at a time into the boiling mixture, using a wide slotted spatula. Allow them to boil for 20 to 25 seconds, then immediately remove with the slotted spatula and place on a prepared baking sheet. Repeat this process until all the pretzels are boiled.

Prepare the egg wash: In a small bowl, whisk together the egg and almond milk and brush generously all over the pretzels with a natural-bristle pastry brush. Sprinkle each with coarse sea salt. Bake for 15 minutes, or until deep golden brown, rotating the pan once for even browning.

Remove from the oven and allow the pretzels to cool just slightly, then brush with melted ghee, if desired, before serving. The pretzels can be stored at room temperature for the first day, or frozen for later use.

ONE-BOWL DINNER ROLLS

These quick and easy dinner rolls are an improvement on the ones already on my blog—this is a true mix-and-bake recipe that makes them perfect to whip up right at dinnertime to go with soup, chili or really anything else you're cooking. Grain-free does not mean bread-free—these rolls have a thick crusty outside and soft chewy inside, and are best served warm from the oven.

Yield: 9 to 10 rolls

1¼ cups (120 g) blanched almond flour

1½ cups (168 g) tapioca flour

5 tbsp (40 g) coconut flour

1 tsp fine sea salt

¾ tsp baking soda

⅓ cup (79 ml) olive oil, plus more for brushing (optional)

⅓ cup (79 ml) water, at room temperature or warmed to 100°F (38°C)

1 tbsp (15 ml) raw apple cider vinegar

2 large eggs, at room temperature

Preheat your oven to 350°F (177°C) and line a large baking sheet with parchment paper.

In a large bowl, combine the almond, tapioca and coconut flours with the salt and baking soda. In a measuring cup, combine the oil, water and vinegar. Make a well in the center of the dry mixture, then stir the wet mixture into the dry with a wooden spoon. Add the eggs and continue to mix with a wooden spoon or silicone spatula to form a dough. Place in the refrigerator to chill for 10 minutes.

Wet your hands a little bit and roll the dough into 2- to 3-inch (5- to 7.5-cm) balls to make 9 or 10 balls. Place them about 2 inches (5 cm) apart on the prepared baking sheet. Lightly brush each roll with a bit of olive oil, if desired, before baking.

Bake for 25 to 30 minutes, or until beginning to turn golden brown. Remove from the oven and allow the rolls to cool for 5 to 10 minutes, then serve them warm.

ACKNOWLEDGMENTS

Ever since I began collecting cookbooks as a young adult, writing one of my own was sort of a pipe dream—a fantasy, really, that seemed far out of reach. It wasn't until I gained confidence with my blog that I (slowly) began to consider that I, too, could write a cookbook one day! And, now that you're reading this, the pipe dream is a reality!

Taking on this project has taught me far more than I imagined it would. I learned that my "stubbornness" and perfectionism have at least *one* purpose, and that seemingly impossible tasks are (usually) possible with the right planning and persistence. I also learned it's possible to live solely on pie for a full week. Just saying.

To my kids—Diana, Emily and Drew. Thank you for putting up with the chaos, frustration and sometimes tears that came with creating this book. A cookbook-writing mom is a hard one to live with! For your very honest taste testing—both the bad and the good reviews—you gave me the confidence I needed to keep going when it got really, really tough.

To my husband Adam, for eating the pie, the cake, the cookies, the bread and so on, and only rarely complaining. You actually *did not* gain the 20 pounds (9 kg) you were certain you would. For always being supportive of my dreams and believing that I could make this book happen. Also, for making sure that kitchen renovation happened *just* in time!

To my mom, for making me believe that anything is possible (because it is!) and for showing me that hard work + a little sweat is nothing to fear—it's the key to making *life* happen. For believing in me from day one, and always loving whatever I bake!

To my dad, for teaching me to honor my creative side and, even more important, instilling in me a love of dessert!

To my sister, for believing that *everything* I do is just the greatest, looking to me for answers to all the big questions and for loving every new thing I bake better than the last.

To Page Street Publishing, for bringing a crazy dream of mine to life, helping me reconnect with my passion for baking and for designing a beautiful cookbook that I'm beyond excited to call my own!

Lastly, to my Paleo Running Momma followers, readers and recipe makers—*you* are essentially what made my dream a reality. Not only do you all give me the confidence and inspiration to keep going, but your feedback over the years has been extremely valuable in creating the recipes for this book. I wouldn't be in this position without you, and I'll be forever grateful of your support and encouragement. Thank you—I love you all!

ABOUT THE AUTHOR

Michele Rosen is the creator, blogger and photographer behind Paleo Running Momma, a food blog with a variety of Paleo recipes for people who don't want to sacrifice their favorite foods while eating a grain-free, dairy-free diet.

While she loves both cooking and baking, she especially finds it rewarding to experiment with Paleo baking recipes—always striving to "crack the code" on a particular recipe, making it as authentic to the original version as possible.

In addition to her passion for healthy cooking and baking, Michele is also a runner who's completed several marathons, including Boston's and New York City's. She has a master's degree in social work from Columbia University and a passion for helping others improve their quality of life through good food, movement and a healthy dose of self-reflection. She also practices yoga and loves to sing—especially while recipe testing. Michele currently lives in Tenafly, New Jersey, with her husband, Adam, and their three children, Diana, Emily and Drew.

INDEX